Printed in Dallas, Texas by The Odee Company

Contact: contact@first15.org
www.first15.org

Designed by Matt Ravenelle
mattravenelle.com

ABOUT FIRST15

Spending time alone with God every day can be a struggle. We're busier – and more stressed – than ever. But still, we know it's important to spend time alone with our Creator. We know we need to read his word, pray, and worship him.

First15 bridges the gap between desire and reality, helping you establish the rhythm of meaningful, daily experiences in God's presence. First15 answers the critical questions:

• Why should I spend time alone with God?
• How do I spend time alone with God?
• How do I get the most out of my time alone with God?
• How can I become more consistent with my time alone with God?

And by answering these questions through the format of daily devotionals, you'll practice the rhythm of meeting with God while experiencing the incredible gift of his loving presence given to those who make time to meet with him.

Allow God's passionate pursuit to draw you in across the next several days. And watch as every day is better than the last as your life is built on the solid foundation of God's love through the power of consistent, meaningful time alone with him.

To learn more about First15, visit our website first15. org. First15 is available across mobile app, email, podcast, and our website. Subscribe to our devotional today and experience God in a fresh way every day.

———————

ABOUT THE AUTHOR

Craig Denison is the author of First15, a daily devotional guiding over a million believers into a fresh experience with God every day. In 2015, Craig founded First15 after sensing a longing in God's heart for his people to be about relationship – real, restored relationship with him – that above all else, he simply wanted the hearts of his people. Craig began praying, dreaming, and writing. And the idea of helping people spend the first fifteen minutes of their day focusing on nothing else but growing in their relationship with God was born. The vision was birthed in Craig's heart that if we as a people would worship, read, and pray at the beginning of every day, everything could change for the better. Craig writes, speaks, and he and his wife, Rachel lead worship to help believers establish a more tangible, meaningful connection with God.

———————

CONTENTS

Trust

"Let us hold fast the confession of our hope without wavering, for he who promised is faithful." Hebrews 10:23

WEEKLY OVERVIEW

Trust is something we are not created to give away lightly. We value trust like we value our own lives, constantly scrutinizing others to see if they're worthy of our trust. But still we are made to do life with help. We are made to place our trust in that which will provide us with more life, joy, and peace. I pray that this week you and I will discover how trustworthy our heavenly Father is. I pray that we will willingly hand over control of our lives to a capable, loving, and near God. And I pray we will experience the abundant life that can only come through placing our trust in a God who gives up everything for relationship with us.

Trustworthy

DEVOTIONAL

Trust is foundational to experiencing the incredible life God offers us in relationship with him. Trust is a commodity of the heart that is only truly given when someone or something proves itself trustworthy. I can only trust you to the measure that I believe you are trustworthy. I can only trust my vehicle to the extent that I believe it will get me somewhere safely.

"In you our fathers trusted; they trusted, and you delivered them. To you they cried and were rescued; in you they trusted and were not put to shame."

PSALM 22:4-5

Scripture makes powerful declarations about those who choose to place their trust in God over the world or themselves. Psalm 22:4-5 says, *"In you our fathers trusted; they trusted, and you delivered them. To you they cried and were rescued; in you they trusted and were not put to shame."* Isaiah 40:31 says, *"But they who wait for the Lord shall renew their strength; they shall mount up with wings like eagles; they shall run and not be weary; they shall walk and not faint."* And Jeremiah 17:7 says simply, *"Blessed is the man who trusts in the Lord, whose trust is the Lord."*

We serve a God who is perfectly trustworthy. We serve a God who *"so loved the world, that he gave his only Son, that whoever believes in him should not perish but have eternal life"* (John 3:16). God has already given us everything. He has done enough to earn our trust. But no matter how trustworthy God is, we still must make the decision to trust him. And no more important decision could be made.

To place our trust in God is to found our lives on the unshakable, powerful, loving, and resourceful character of our heavenly Father. He alone has the ability to provide for us, heal us, love us, empower us, and save us. He alone is one to trust. When we place our hope in him, we anchor our lives, emotions, finances, relationships, and future in a God who wholly cares for us, loves us, and promises to provide for us.

God promises you in Isaiah 41:10, *"Fear not, for I am with you; be not dismayed, for I am your God; I will strengthen you, I will help you, I will uphold you with my righteous right hand."* You do not have to go through life on your own. You do not have to carve out your own way. You do not have to work to be loved, liked, or provided for. When you place your trust in God, give him your heart, and follow him, you will discover a wealth of abundant life unseen by those living for the world. The Creator of all, the Author and Perfecter of your faith, is beckoning you to place your trust in him alone. He is beckoning you to stop looking to the world and yourself for that which only he can truly and consistently provide. Place your trust in him alone today and experience a peace and joy that comes from casting off the weight you were never made to carry.

15

GUIDED PRAYER

1. Meditate on the trustworthiness of your heavenly Father. Allow Scripture to stir up your faith to place your trust in God alone.

"For God so loved the world, that he gave his only Son, that whoever believes in him should not perish but have eternal life." John 3:16

"Be strong and courageous. Do not fear or be in dread of them, for it is the Lord your God who goes with you. He will not leave you or forsake you." Deuteronomy 31:6

"Fear not, for I am with you; be not dismayed, for I am your God; I will strengthen you, I will help you, I will uphold you with my righteous right hand." Isaiah 41:10

2. Who or what are you placing your trust in? Who do you see as your provider, source of happiness, or foundation for your future?

3. Place your trust in God alone. Cast the cares of your life on his shoulders and receive his sustaining peace. Rest in his wonderful presence in faith that he will truly take care of you.

"Blessed is the man who trusts in the Lord, whose trust is the Lord." Jeremiah 17:7

"In you our fathers trusted; they trusted, and you delivered them. To you they cried and were rescued; in you they trusted and were not put to shame." Psalm 22:4-5

"Trust in the Lord with all your heart, and do not lean on your own understanding. In all your ways acknowledge him, and he will make straight your paths. Be not wise in your own eyes; fear the Lord, and turn away from evil. It will be healing to your flesh and refreshment to your bones." Proverbs 3:5-8

May Matthew 11:28-30 lead you to a lifestyle of rest and peace through trust in your good Father:

Come to me, all who labor and are heavy laden, and I will give you rest. Take my yoke upon you, and learn from me, for I am gentle and lowly in heart, and you will find rest for your souls. For my yoke is easy, and my burden is light.

Extended Reading: Psalm 107

Obedience

DAY 2

DEVOTIONAL

Throughout our lives we are commanded to obey. Whether it be a parent telling us, "Pick that up," or, "Don't do that," or a government laying down a law, we acknowledge obedience as a necessary part of life. And so often because we grow up with some sense of the purpose of obedience, we apply our worldly notions of obedience to our relationship with God. We see the commands of Scripture or feel a prompting from the Spirit and sense a similar tone of command.

*"If you are willing and obedient,
you shall eat the good of the land."*

ISAIAH 1:19

The problem with carrying a worldly notion of obedience into our relationship with God is that no one, no matter how loving, can or will fully care for us the way our heavenly Father does. No matter how good the lawmaker, parent, friend, or teacher, no one truly knows the future like God does.

Isaiah 1:19 promises us, *"If you are willing and obedient, you shall eat the good of the land."* God asks for us to be obedient to him because his plan is always for our betterment. He sees what lies ahead of us. He knows the potential perils or fruits of our actions. And like a Good Shepherd, he longs to guide us into an incredibly abundant life filled with all the goodness of his kingdom.

If we are ever going to experience the wealth of glorious inheritance God has for us, we must learn to trust him and obey. God cannot lead us to still waters and plentiful pastures if we are unwilling to follow him. He cannot lead us into the depths of his love if we don't trust in his loving-kindness. He cannot lead us into consistent encounters with him if we don't trust that he is as near as his word promises. And he cannot satisfy the deep desires of our hearts if we don't trust that his purposes for us will truly satiate our longings.

1 Samuel 15:22 says, *"Has the Lord as great delight in burnt offerings and sacrifices, as in obeying the voice of the Lord? Behold, to obey is better than sacrifice, and to listen than the fat of rams."* God longs to fashion us into children who are quick to obey him. He earnestly desires our obedience because he earnestly desires abundant life that only comes through acting upon a foundational trust in his goodness.

Take time in guided prayer to think about reasons why you aren't fully obeying God's word or the promptings of his Spirit. What doubt do you have in your heart? Why don't you fully trust that he will completely satisfy your deepest longings? Make space to rest in his presence and trust that he is who he says he is. Trust that he will do what he has promised. May you experience the abundant life that comes through total obedience to your loving heavenly Father.

GUIDED PRAYER

1. Meditate on the importance of obedience. Allow Scripture to fill you with a desire to obey God sooner and to greater measures.

"Why do you call me 'Lord, Lord,' and not do what I tell you?" Luke 6:46

"If you are willing and obedient, you shall eat the good of the land." Isaiah 1:19

"Has the Lord as great delight in burnt offerings and sacrifices, as in obeying the voice of the Lord? Behold, to obey is better than sacrifice, and to listen than the fat of rams." 1 Samuel 15:22

2. Why do you have a hard time obeying God's word or his promptings? In what ways do you not trust him?

3. Reflect on his promises in those areas and place your trust in him. Rest in his presence and experience his wonderful character. Ask him to reveal how trustworthy he is that you might place your trust more fully in him today.

"This Book of the Law shall not depart from your mouth, but you shall meditate on it day and night, so that you may be careful to do according to all that is written in it. For then you will make your way prosperous, and then you will have good success." Joshua 1:8

"Every good gift and every perfect gift is from above, coming down from the Father of lights with whom there is no variation or shadow due to change." James 1:17

"For you know the grace of our Lord Jesus Christ, that though he was rich, yet for your sake he became poor, so that you by his poverty might become rich." 2 Corinthians 8:9

Placing our trust in someone is always a process. God does not assume that you will fully trust him until you truly get to know him. To know his love and kindness in a way that will result in trust takes time spent daily developing your relationship. If you want to experience the fruit of obedience and trust, you must make time to get to know your heavenly Father. In a moment where you feel like going your own way, you must have a solid foundation built on knowing the goodness of God and his word. Have patience with yourself and center your life around developing a greater relationship with your heavenly Father. May you come to know the heart of God as described in Ephesians 3:17-19:

That you, being rooted and grounded in love, may have strength to comprehend with all the saints what is the breadth and length and height and depth, and to know the love of Christ that surpasses knowledge, that you may be filled with all the fullness of God.

Extended Reading: 1 Peter 1

21

Understanding

DAY 3

DEVOTIONAL

True understanding about ourselves, others, and this
life only comes through trust in God. God alone has
perspective and truth. God alone has understanding
about what matters, who we are, and what will happen.
And the good news for you and me today is that our

"Trust in the Lord with all your heart, and
do not lean on your own understanding."

PROVERBS 3:5

heavenly Father is absolutely longing to share his understanding. God yearns for us to think and see through the lens of the Holy Spirit and his word. Proverbs 3:5-8 says,

Trust in the Lord with all your heart, and do not lean on your own understanding. In all your ways acknowledge him, and he will make straight your paths. Be not wise in your own eyes; fear the Lord, and turn away from evil. It will be healing to your flesh and refreshment to your bones.

Why is it that when Scripture promises us God's understanding we still do life apart from his wisdom? Why do we look to our own minds and go our own ways when God makes his understanding and will so available? You and I are only capable of looking for understanding in that which we fully trust. If we don't trust that God's wisdom and will are truly the best path laid before us, we will go our own ways. If we don't trust that God's commands will actually produce the most abundant life, we will choose the ways of the world. To live with godly understanding and wisdom is to look to God alone as our Truth.

Proverbs 3:13-18 stirs my heart to lean on God for my understanding. Scripture says,

Blessed is the one who finds wisdom, and the one who gets understanding, for the gain from her is better than gain from silver and her profit better than gold. She is more precious than jewels, and nothing you desire can compare with her. Long life is in her right hand; in her left hand are riches and honor. Her ways are ways of pleasantness, and all her paths are peace. She is a tree of life to those who lay hold of her; those who hold her fast are called blessed.

While all the world is declaring to you its understanding of truth, I pray that you will look to its One, True Source today. I pray that you will lean on your loving heavenly Father for understanding about yourself, your life, and others. May today be marked by a continual overflow of revelation. May you know how God feels about you and base your image off his understanding. May you experience to greater depths the perfect mind of Jesus. And may God's word transform your life as it plants seeds of wisdom that grow into beautiful, plentiful trees of peace and life.

23

GUIDED PRAYER

1. Meditate on the availability of God's understanding. Allow Scripture to stir up a desire to lean on your heavenly Father for truth and wisdom.

"My son, if you receive my words and treasure up my commandments with you, making your ear attentive to wisdom and inclining your heart to understanding; yes, if you call out for insight and raise your voice for understanding, if you seek it like silver and search for it as for hidden treasures, then you will understand the fear of the Lord and find the knowledge of God." Proverbs 2:1-5

"Trust in the Lord with all your heart, and do not lean on your own understanding. In all your ways acknowledge him, and he will make straight your paths. Be not wise in your own eyes; fear the Lord, and turn away from evil. It will be healing to your flesh and refreshment to your bones." Proverbs 3:5-8

2. In what ways do you lean on yourself or something of the world for understanding and truth? What do you look to for your perspectives and source of value?

3. Take time to lean on God for his understanding. Search out Scripture and the Spirit for wisdom and understanding concerning yourself, your life, and others. Ask him to help you be one who seeks understanding from him in every area. Take time to rest in his presence and discover the wealth of his affections for you.

"The unfolding of your words gives light; it imparts understanding to the simple." Psalm 119:130

"Let not the wise man boast in his wisdom, let not the mighty man boast in his might, let not the rich man boast in his riches, but let him who boasts boast in this, that he understands and knows me, that I am the Lord who practices steadfast love, justice, and righteousness in the earth. For in these things I delight, declares the Lord." Jeremiah 9:23-24

"The purpose in a man's heart is like deep water, but a man of understanding will draw it out." Proverbs 20:5

Paul's prayer in Colossians 1:9-10 is my prayer for you. May your life bear the fruit of heavenly understanding today:

And so, from the day we heard, we have not ceased to pray for you, asking that you may be filled with the knowledge of his will in all spiritual wisdom and understanding, so as to walk in a manner worthy of the Lord, fully pleasing to him, bearing fruit in every good work and increasing in the knowledge of God.

Extended Reading: Proverbs 3

Plans

DAY 4

DEVOTIONAL

Our plans are one of the areas of life in which it can be most difficult to trust God. So often we look within ourselves to discover desires and ambitions and form plans based solely on our understanding and limited perspective. We place the weight of planning our lives squarely on our own shoulders and settle for a life filled with pressure and failure. Our heavenly Father is speaking

*"Many are the plans in the mind of a man, but
it is the purpose of the Lord that will stand."*

PROVERBS 19:21

over his children his great desire to guide us. He longs to share his wonderful plans with us that will satisfy the deepest desires of our hearts and help us store up bountiful treasure in heaven with him.

James 4:13-15 illustrates the necessity of looking to God for our plans:

Come now, you who say, "Today or tomorrow we will go into such and such a town and spend a year there and trade and make a profit"— yet you do not know what tomorrow will bring. What is your life? For you are a mist that appears for a little time and then vanishes. Instead you ought to say, "If the Lord wills, we will live and do this or that."

Why do we look to ourselves when we *"do not know what tomorrow will bring"*? Why do look to our own will when our heavenly Father longs to share his perfect will with us? For some of us, we simply don't know that God wants to reveal his plans to us. So many believers are living without the revelation of all that's available to them through the life, death, and resurrection of Jesus. Know today God's heart for you. You can know his plans for you. He is a good Father who longs to shepherd you into the greater things of this life.

For others of us that know God wants to share his plans with us, we fail to look for or follow his leadership because somewhere in our hearts we doubt that he will truly give us the best life. We look at the lives of other believers and decide we'll have more fun if we go our own way. So often, we as Christians have not exhibited to others a lifestyle of being fully satisfied in God and his plans. We exhibit a lukewarm faith where we neither experience the fullness of God or what the world has to offer. And as a result, our lives are lived without passion, joy, or abundance in any form.

The truth of God's heart for you and me today is that he has perfect, pleasing plans for us that he longs to reveal. Proverbs 3:5-6 says, *"Trust in the Lord with all your heart, and do not lean on your own understanding. In all your ways acknowledge him, and he will make straight your paths."* God longs to make straight the paths laid before you. He longs to guide you into greater and greater things in every season. He knows what lies ahead of you. He knows opportunities and roadblocks that are coming your way. And he is the Good Shepherd who will lead you into the fullness of life available to you this side of heaven. May you trust your loving heavenly Father with your plans and experience his leadership in every decision you face today.

GUIDED PRAYER

1. Meditate on the availability and fruit of trusting God with your plans.

"For I know the plans I have for you, declares the Lord, plans for welfare and not for evil, to give you a future and a hope." Jeremiah 29:11

"Trust in the Lord with all your heart, and do not lean on your own understanding. In all your ways acknowledge him, and he will make straight your paths." Proverbs 3:5-6

2. What keeps you from trusting God with your plans? Why do you look to yourself to plan your own way?

"Come now, you who say, 'Today or tomorrow we will go into such and such a town and spend a year there and trade and make a profit'— yet you do not know what tomorrow will bring. What is your life? For you are a mist that appears for a little time and then vanishes. Instead you ought to say, 'If the Lord wills, we will live and do this or that.'" James 4:13-15

3. Lay your plans before your Good Shepherd and ask him for his plans. Look to his plans for your work, family, and relationships. Ask him how he has plans to satisfy the desires of your heart for joy, passion, and purpose.

"Delight yourself in the Lord, and he will give you the desires of your heart." Psalm 37:4

"Therefore do not be foolish, but understand what the will of the Lord is." Ephesians 5:17

"The Lord will fulfill his purpose for me; your steadfast love, O Lord, endures forever. Do not forsake the work of your hands." Psalm 138:8

God is more concerned about the state of your heart than the work of your hands. Romans 14:17 says, *"For the kingdom of God is not a matter of eating and drinking but of righteousness and peace and joy in the Holy Spirit."* Of course God cares about what you do. But before he longs for you to accomplish his plans for you, he simply wants you to know his love. You serve a God who cares about your emotions, thoughts, perspectives, and sense of worth. More than he wants you to do something, he wants you to be something. He longs for your life to be a reflection of his overwhelming love and goodness. He longs for your life to be a declaration of his grace and nearness. Look to God for your satisfaction and follow the desires he places in your heart. May the work of your hands and the state of your heart be centered on the goodness of your loving, powerful, and near heavenly Father.

Extended Reading: Proverbs 19

Emotions

DAY 5

DEVOTIONAL

Do you know that God cares deeply about your emotions? Your heavenly Father longs for your life to be marked by emotional joy, fulfillment, satisfaction, and peace. He longs for your emotions to be rooted and grounded in his steadfast love and goodness. Our God is an emotional God. He is not void of feelings. We feel because he feels. We have emotions because we are made in his image.

*"For our heart is glad in him,
because we trust in his holy name."*

PSALM 33:21

For much of my Christian life I thought my emotions had to be based on my circumstances. I felt happy or sad based on others' opinions, the pressures of life, and opportunities I had or didn't have. As a result I was on a constant emotional roller coaster following the ups and downs of this shaky world. I found myself controlled by the things of the world rather than the foundation of love laid before me by the sacrificial love of Jesus.

Scripture continually describes a link between emotional health and trust. Isaiah 26:3-4 says, *"You keep him in perfect peace whose mind is stayed on you, because he trusts in you. Trust in the Lord forever, for the Lord God is an everlasting rock."* Psalm 56:3-4 says, *"When I am afraid, I put my trust in you. In God, whose word I praise, in God I trust; I shall not be afraid. What can flesh do to me?"* And Psalm 33:21 says, *"For our heart is glad in him, because we trust in his holy name."*

We are robbed of having our emotions rooted in God whenever we take on more pressure than we are meant to carry. Our emotional health is directly linked to our level of trust. We feel pressure at work when we look to our job and co-workers for our provision, identity, purpose, and fulfillment. We feel pressure in our relationships when our worth isn't based on God's perspective but the opinions of others. We are robbed of peace when we try and plan our own steps rather than following our Good Shepherd into the green pastures and still waters.

In John 14:27 Jesus says, *"Peace I leave with you; my peace I give to you. Not as the world gives do I give to you. Let not your hearts be troubled, neither let them be afraid."* God's heart is to fill you with peace. He longs for you to have all the fruit of the Spirit dwelling within you. He has consistent, constant peace available to you. But you must trust him in every area of your life. You must hand over the reins of your relationships, job, identity, and plans to your Good Shepherd. You must trust that he will guide you perfectly into an abundant life.

Look to your heavenly Father for peace. Find rest in his abundant love. Find your self-worth in the fact that God so desired relationship with you that he laid down his own life to have it. Your Father counts you worthy of the death of his only Son. Trust him today. Place your entire life in his capable hands. And experience abundant life in the area of your emotions, rooting and grounding yourself in his unconditional, available love. May your life be marked by increasing emotional health as you grow in trust.

GUIDED PRAYER

1. Meditate on the link between trust and emotional health. Allow Scripture to stir up your desire and willingness to trust God with every area of your life.

"For our heart is glad in him, because we trust in his holy name." Psalm 33:21

"When I am afraid, I put my trust in you. In God, whose word I praise, in God I trust; I shall not be afraid. What can flesh do to me?" Psalm 56:3-4

2. Where are you not experiencing abundant life in your emotions? Where are you void of peace, joy, passion, and purpose?

3. Ask God to help you discern what part of your life you are not trusting to him. Hand over that area to him and find peace and rest in his trustworthiness.

"You keep him in perfect peace whose mind is stayed on you, because he trusts in you. Trust in the Lord forever, for the Lord God is an everlasting rock." Isaiah 26:3-4

"Do not be anxious about anything, but in everything by prayer and supplication with thanksgiving let your requests be made known to God. And the peace of God, which surpasses all understanding, will guard your hearts and your minds in Christ Jesus." Philippians 4:6-7

"Peace I leave with you; my peace I give to you. Not as the world gives do I give to you. Let not your hearts be troubled, neither let them be afraid." John 14:27

Don't settle for less than Jesus died to give you. Your life can be completely wrapped up in God's presence, unconditional love, and ability to guide you. You can be filled with the emotions of God. Don't settle for pressure, stress, anger, and frustration. Don't settle for sadness, insecurity, or depression. Place your trust in God, open your heart, and receive the peace that can only come from your life being hidden in the heart of your perfect heavenly Father.

Extended Reading: John 14

Provision

DAY 6

DEVOTIONAL

We serve a God who abundantly provides for us everything we could ever need. There are so many Scriptures about God's promise of provision. There are so many stories of God breaking through when his people needed him and providing exceedingly. We have a good Father who longs for his children to experience the peace and joy that comes from trusting in his desire to provide.

> *"I have been young, and now am old, yet I have not seen the righteous forsaken or his children begging for bread. He is ever lending generously, and his children become a blessing."*

PSALM 37:25-26

The famous Psalm 23 begins in a way that perfectly illustrates the heart of one who trusts in God. Psalm 23:1 says, *"The Lord is my shepherd; I shall not want."* Let those words sink in for a second. What would it be like to go through life with the peace and security that comes from wholeheartedly believing you *"shall not want"*? How would you approach work, finances, and relationships if you knew you would never want?

Abundant peace and security is available for you today if you will trust in your heavenly Father's promise to provide everything you need. He is a God of grace who loves you. You will not want in this life or for all of eternity.

Allow these Scriptures to stir up your faith and trust in your heavenly Father: *"I have been young, and now am old, yet I have not seen the righteous forsaken or his children begging for bread. He is ever lending generously, and his children become a blessing"* (Psalm 37:25-26). *"Look at the birds of the air: they neither sow nor reap nor gather into barns, and yet your heavenly Father feeds them. Are you not of more value than they?"* (Matthew 6:26). *"And my God will supply every need of yours according to his riches in glory in Christ Jesus"* (Philippians 4:19).

A large part of trusting God in the area of provision is aligning your desires with his. Trust that he will provide the absolute best life you can live. Whether he provides abundantly in the eyes of the world does not matter. He is a perfect, loving Father who has absolutely perfect plans for you. If you are truly seeking him and trusting him with all your heart, you will live the best life possible. He knows what you need. He knows the desires within you. Stop looking to the world for examples of what your life should look like and seek his will above all else. Look to loving him and being loved by him as the best thing in life and all else will fall into place. May your life be marked by the abundant provision of your loving Father today in all areas as you place your trust in him.

GUIDED PRAYER

1. Meditate on God's desire to abundantly provide for you. Allow Scripture to stir up trust in God's provision.

"The Lord is my shepherd; I shall not want." Psalm 23:1

"Look at the birds of the air: they neither sow nor reap nor gather into barns, and yet your heavenly Father feeds them. Are you not of more value than they?" Matthew 6:26

"I have been young, and now am old, yet I have not seen the righteous forsaken or his children begging for bread. He is ever lending generously, and his children become a blessing." Psalm 37:25-26

2. Where are you not experiencing the peace that comes from trusting in the provision of your heavenly Father? Where are you seeking more than what is best for you? Where are you looking to the world as your example of a good life rather than seeking out the heart of God?

"Keep your life free from love of money, and be content with what you have, for he has said, 'I will never leave you nor forsake you.'" Hebrews 13:5

"For the sun rises with its scorching heat and withers the grass; its flower falls, and its beauty perishes. So also will the rich man fade away in the midst of his pursuits." James 1:11

3. Place your trust for provision in your heavenly Father alone. Take the weight of provision off your own shoulders and place it squarely on his. Stop looking to others or to circumstances to give you what you need. Look to God alone. Rest in his peace and love as you settle into a lifestyle of trusting him.

"And my God will supply every need of yours according to his riches in glory in Christ Jesus." Philippians 4:19

2 Corinthians 9:8-11 lays out God's plan to provide for you abundantly so that others might be blessed through you. May you be used by God today to be an example of his heart to provide. May what he has given you create an overflow of love and sacrifice for others:

And God is able to make all grace abound to you, so that having all sufficiency in all things at all times, you may abound in every good work. As it is written, "He has distributed freely, he has given to the poor; his righteousness endures forever." He who supplies seed to the sower and bread for food will supply and multiply your seed for sowing and increase the harvest of your righteousness. You will be enriched in every way to be generous in every way, which through us will produce thanksgiving to God.

Extended Reading: Psalm 37

Sanctification

DAY 7

DEVOTIONAL

Sanctification and holiness are words that used to strike terror into my heart. As a believer I have always tried to pursue holiness, and I always seem to fail. It seems like no matter what I do I can't escape sin and can't get past my own brokenness and mess. Even in seasons where I am

"Commit your way to the Lord; trust in him, and he will act. He will bring forth your righteousness as the light, and your justice as the noonday."

PSALM 37:5-6

experiencing freedom from some sins, there always seems to be something else I need to fix or get better at. I've felt like I was on this endless tightrope of spiritual development that I kept falling off of and of which I couldn't seem to find the end.

While God's heart is most definitely for our sanctification and holiness, his perspective is far different than what I just described. You see, God knows that sanctification doesn't come about through our efforts. I can in no way sanctify myself because in and of myself I have no holiness. The truth God has for us today is simply this: sanctification comes about by true relationship with our heavenly Father alone. Holiness is the direct result of openly and continually encountering the nature of a perfect, loving, and available God.

If we are going to experience the fruit of righteousness, we must learn to trust God in his plan for our sanctification. We must learn to trust that in encountering him we will experience freedom from our sin and healing for the wounds that drive us to the things of the world.

Psalm 37:5-6 says, *"Commit your way to the Lord; trust in him, and he will act. He will bring forth your righteousness as the light, and your justice as the noonday."* When we

trust God to bring about our righteousness by simply committing our way to him and trusting in him, we engage in a process of sanctification founded on encounters with his loving grace.

Sanctification is not meant to be this heady process of turmoil and striving that we so often experience. While it may be difficult, it is designed to be filled with the continually forgiving and loving heart of our good Father. It is designed to be based on experiencing Jesus that we might become more like him.

Spend time today seeking the heart of your heavenly Father. Commit your ways to him and trust in him. Ask him to reveal his heart for your righteousness. Ask him to guide you into a process of sanctification marked by his grace, love, and nearness. Stop seeing the process of sanctification as a never-ending timeline and instead center it wholly around relationship with your heavenly Father. May you experience righteousness and holiness today as you encounter the perfect nature of Jesus. May your day be marked by peace as you commit your spiritual development to the hands of the Potter. And may you be transformed into the image of Jesus as you engage in the process of sanctification based on relationship with a good, near God.

39

GUIDED PRAYER

1. Meditate on the process of sanctification. Allow God's heart as described in Scripture to stir up your desire to engage in relationship-based sanctification.

"Commit your way to the Lord; trust in him, and he will act. He will bring forth your righteousness as the light, and your justice as the noonday." Psalm 37:5-6

"Therefore, if anyone is in Christ, he is a new creation. The old has passed away; behold, the new has come." 2 Corinthians 5:17

"I have been crucified with Christ. It is no longer I who live, but Christ who lives in me. And the life I now live in the flesh I live by faith in the Son of God, who loved me and gave himself for me." Galatians 2:20

2. In what ways have you been striving for your own righteousness and holiness rather than receiving it from God? In what ways have you been looking at sanctification as a timeline or tightrope rather than as a relationship with a good God?

"I do not nullify the grace of God, for if righteousness were through the law, then Christ died for no purpose." Galatians 2:21

3. Take time to encounter the holiness of your loving Father. Open your heart and receive his presence. And in his presence commit to him the process of your sanctification. Allow peace and rest to fill your heart as the burden of striving for sanctification falls off in light of God's glorious grace.

"But as he who called you is holy, you also be holy in all your conduct." 1 Peter 1:15

"In the year that King Uzziah died I saw the Lord sitting upon a throne, high and lifted up; and the train of his robe filled the temple. Above him stood the seraphim. Each had six wings: with two he covered his face, and with two he covered his feet, and with two he flew. And one called to another and said: 'Holy, holy, holy is the Lord of hosts; the whole earth is full of his glory!' And the foundations of the thresholds shook at the voice of him who called, and the house was filled with smoke. And I said: 'Woe is me! For I am lost; for I am a man of unclean lips, and I dwell in the midst of a people of unclean lips; for my eyes have seen the King, the Lord of hosts!'" Isaiah 6:1-5

I pray that 2 Peter 1:2-4 will fill you with the courage to have grace and rest in the process of sanctification. May your life be marked by God's forgiveness and grace.

May grace and peace be multiplied to you in the knowledge of God and of Jesus our Lord. His divine power has granted to us all things that pertain to life and godliness, through the knowledge of him who called us to his own glory and excellence, by which he has granted to us his precious and very great promises, so that through them you may become partakers of the divine nature, having escaped from the corruption that is in the world because of sinful desire.

Extended Reading: 1 Peter 1

God's promises

"For all the promises of
God find their Yes in him."
2 Corinthians 1:20

WEEKLY OVERVIEW

There is only one constant in this ever-changing world, and that's the character of our heavenly Father. The very earth itself is undergoing changes constantly. What seems the most immovable now will one day be done away with. But God is unchanging. God is unwavering. He's completely faithful and committed to seeing through the promises he's made you. As we look this week at the promises of God may you ground yourself in his unchanging love. May God's character become your source and refuge—your constant and unshakable foundation.

God Promises His Will

DAY 8

DEVOTIONAL

In the life of Jesus, God illustrated not only his nearness to us, but his desire to co-labor with us in his plans of redemption for all peoples, all generations and all of creation. And within God's desire to partner with us on the earth lies an incredible promise he makes to his people: God promises to share with us the knowledge of his will. An incredible example of God sharing his will with his people is displayed in Ephesians 1:7-12:

*"Making known to us the mystery of his will,
according to his purpose, which he set forth in Christ
as a plan for the fullness of time, to unite all things
in him, things in heaven and things on earth."*

EPHESIANS 1:9-10

In him we have redemption through his blood, the forgiveness of our trespasses, according to the riches of his grace, which he lavished upon us, in all wisdom and insight making known to us the mystery of his will, according to his purpose, which he set forth in Christ as a plan for the fullness of time, to unite all things in him, things in heaven and things on earth. In him we have obtained an inheritance, having been predestined according to the purpose of him who works all things according to the counsel of his will, so that we who were the first to hope in Christ might be to the praise of his glory.

Paul tells us that God, through the death of Jesus, revealed the mystery of his will to his people. Jesus' death tells us of God's incredible plan to reconcile everything around us to himself. God's plan set throughout the ages revealed itself in Jesus' actions. However, Scripture doesn't only describe a single time God revealed the mystery of his will. The Bible is clear that God desires for his people to continually know his will.

Romans 12:1-2 says, *"I appeal to you therefore, brothers, by the mercies of God, to present your bodies as a living sacrifice, holy and acceptable to God, which is your spiritual worship. Do not be conformed to this world, but be transformed by the renewal of your mind, that by testing you may discern what is the will of God, what is good and acceptable and perfect."* In the renewing of your mind to God's truth, you position yourself to continually discern the *"good and acceptable and perfect"* will of God. How amazing! Not only does God want you to know his will, but he's given you an incredible tool to do so in the renewing of your mind.

Take time today to seek his will through Scripture, listening to the Holy Spirit and seeking counsel from those who are in tune with God's heart. Allow him to reveal his will in whatever way he desires. Spend time in his presence letting him reveal the desires of his heart. And align yourself with his unceasing faithfulness as he speaks and leads you throughout your day. May you discern the *"good and acceptable and perfect"* will of God today as you spend time in guided prayer.

49

GUIDED PRAYER

1. Meditate on God's desire to share with you the knowledge of his will.

"Making known to us the mystery of his will, according to his purpose, which he set forth in Christ as a plan for the fullness of time, to unite all things in him, things in heaven and things on earth." Ephesians 1:9-10

2. Where in your life do you need God's guidance? Where do you need direction?

3. Ask God to give you the knowledge of his will. Listen for him to direct you right now. Pay attention to any Scripture that come to mind. Trust that God speaks and wants you to know his will.

"I appeal to you therefore, brothers, by the mercies of God, to present your bodies as a living sacrifice, holy and acceptable to God, which is your spiritual worship. Do not be conformed to this world, but be transformed by the renewal of your mind, that by testing you may discern what is the will of God, what is good and acceptable and perfect." Romans 12:1-2

God wants to speak to you throughout your day, influencing the various decisions you make. Your heavenly Father loves you. As a good Father, he longs to share with you what's best for you, and he'll do so in the best way possible. Trust and listen today, and live your life in response to the life-giving knowledge of God's will.

Extended Reading: Romans 12

God Promises
His Strength

DEVOTIONAL

Creator God in his infinite wisdom and love chose to create mankind knowing full well that we would choose our ways over his. We're made with a terrible capacity to live out of our own strength. As a result, we see in both Scripture and our own lives incredible failures—examples of our collective weakness played out before our very eyes. We see it in the declining morality of society. We see it in the very lives of those around us that just can't seem to get

it together. Weakness seems to be threaded into the very fabric of our world. The world is plagued by the weakness of those who inhabit it.

But, the Bible also contains incredible stories of the victories of God's people. The list goes on and on: Moses and the Egyptians, David and Goliath, Samson and the Philistines, and the early church spreading the gospel across the world despite insurmountable

> *"Fear not, for I am with you; be not dismayed, for
> I am your God; I will strengthen you, I will help you,
> I will uphold you with my righteous right hand."*

ISAIAH 41:10

odds. And along with all the stories of victory, Scripture also contains many stories of failure. So, what made the difference? What separates the stories of success from the stories of failure? The difference is found in the people of God allowing God to be their strength. Success in Scripture came solely when God was made strong in man's weakness.

Psalm 103:13-14 says, *"As a father shows compassion to his children, so the Lord shows compassion to those who fear him. For he knows our frame; he remembers that we are dust."* God created us. He knows our weakness. He knows that apart from him we can do nothing. But the beauty of the gospel is that as believers we are no longer apart from him. Through the death of Jesus, we are now one with Christ, wrapped up in his story of redemption. We have been saved from having to do life on our own, in our own strength.

Your heavenly Father says to you today, *"Fear not, for I am with you; be not dismayed, for I am your God; I will strengthen you, I will help you, I will uphold you with my righteous right hand"* (Isaiah 41:10). Your God is the same God of David, Samson, Paul, and John. The success that they had was the direct result of their choosing God's strength over their own. Paul wrote in

2 Corinthians 12:9, *"But he said to me, 'My grace is sufficient for you, for my power is made perfect in weakness.' Therefore I will boast all the more gladly of my weaknesses, so that the power of Christ may rest upon me."* Paul chose to boast of his weakness because he knew of the steadfast strength of God in his own life. He knew that his success was solely by the strength of his God.

Your heavenly Father promises his strength to you today. Just as he worked to help Paul spread the gospel, just as he helped David slay the giant Goliath, he desires to help you today in whatever lies ahead. Acknowledge your weakness but at the same time, hold fast to the the knowledge of the incredible strength of your heavenly Father. Deuteronomy 31:6 says, *"He will not leave you or forsake you."* The strength of God is always with you. All you have to do is choose his ways over your own. Live in light of the revelation of your own weakness and God's strength, and you will experience the power of the Creator of the universe working directly in your own life.

Where do you need God's strength? What area of your life seems to be plagued by weakness? Ask God to work in your life, and experience the fruit of co-laboring with your heavenly Father today.

54

GUIDED PRAYER

1. Reflect on your own weakness. What situations in your life seem to be without the strength of God?

"As a father shows compassion to his children, so the Lord shows compassion to those who fear him. For he knows our frame; he remembers that we are dust." Psalm 103:13-14

2. Now meditate on God's desire to be strong in your weakness. Think about stories of people in the Bible who did incredible things solely by the strength of God.

"But he said to me, 'My grace is sufficient for you, for my power is made perfect in weakness.' Therefore I will boast all the more gladly of my weaknesses, so that the power of Christ may rest upon me." 2 Corinthians 12:9

3. Ask God to be strong in your weakness today. Ask the Spirit to guide you and work in any and every situation you find yourself in. Ask him to guide your words, actions, mindsets and emotions that you might live entirely in his strength.

"Fear not, for I am with you; be not dismayed, for I am your God; I will strengthen you, I will help you, I will uphold you with my righteous right hand." Isaiah 41:10

How incredible is the heart of God that he would choose to share with us his own strength! Your God cares for you so deeply that he desires to work closely and effectively in your life. The very strength that formed the mountains, parted the seas and sustains every living thing is available to you today. Rest in God's promise that he is not distant. You have a strong God who loves you and is for you. Live today experiencing the peace and power of God's strength made strong in your weakness.

Extended Reading: Psalm 103

God Promises His Compassion

DAY 10

DEVOTIONAL

Compassion is something seldom experienced in a world filled with indifference and cruelty. Most people don't seem to possess the level of selflessness compassion requires. Our society makes it clear that our acceptance has everything to do with our success and little to do with the grace and compassion of others for us. How we are loved and respected is based on our accomplishments and abilities rather than the love and compassion of those around us. But our God is not of this world.

"'For the mountains may depart and the hills be removed, but my steadfast love shall not depart from you, and my covenant of peace shall not be removed,' says the Lord, who has compassion on you."

ISAIAH 54:10

In Isaiah 54:10, God gives us his beautiful promise of compassion, *"'For the mountains may depart and the hills be removed, but my steadfast love shall not depart from you, and my covenant of peace shall not be removed,' says the Lord, who has compassion on you."* The love of your heavenly Father is steadfast and immovable. His compassion for you is more sure than the very ground you walk on. And what's more, your God's compassion is tethered together with his grace. Psalm 103:8 says, *"The Lord is compassionate and gracious, slow to anger, abounding in love"* (NIV). God's compassion is not the result of what you do, but instead the direct result of his boundless love for you.

God's love is foundationally different than the love of others. In a world founded on the notion of works and rewards, cause and effect—God wants to build your foundation on his unconditional compassion. God longs to establish your relationship on the building blocks of his love and grace. It was God's compassion for you that drove him to send Jesus to his death. It was God's compassion for you that led him to search you out when sin had wedged a great

chasm between you. And it's God's compassion that drives him even now to pour out his unfathomable love and affection over you.

Where in your life do you need to experience God's promise of compassion? Where do you feel like you don't measure up? Where do you feel unloved? Isaiah 30:18-19 says,

Therefore the Lord waits to be gracious to you, and therefore he exalts himself to show mercy to you. For the Lord is a God of justice; blessed are all those who wait for him. For a people shall dwell in Zion, in Jerusalem; you shall weep no more. He will surely be gracious to you at the sound of your cry. As soon as he hears it, he answers you.

Cry out to your God today. You can place your trust in his compassion. His love will not fail you. Again, *"He will surely be gracious to you at the sound of your cry. As soon as he hears it, he answers you."* Rest in his promise of compassion. Let his love build you up in all of the areas where the world has torn you down. May the foundation of your life be built on the promise of God's limitless grace and compassion.

57

GUIDED PRAYER

1. Meditate on God's promise of compassion.

"'For the mountains may depart and the hills be removed, but my steadfast love shall not depart from you, and my covenant of peace shall not be removed,' says the Lord, who has compassion on you." Isaiah 54:10

2. Now reflect on your own life. Where do you need to experience the compassion of God? Where do you feel unloved?

3. Ask God to pour out his love on those areas of your life. Ask God to reveal his heart of compassion for you. Choose to see yourself as God does.

"The Lord is compassionate and gracious, slow to anger, abounding in love" Psalm 103:8 (NIV)

One of the most important things you can do to live out the abundant life God intends for you is to align your perspective with God's. The world will always tell you that you aren't good enough. Choosing to see yourself as you perceive those around you do will only set you up for heartache. You can choose to view yourself with the same grace and compassion that God does—today. He sees you perfectly. He sees you truthfully. And he sees you lovingly. Whenever you feel like you need God's compassion, go back to the truth of what his word says. His promises are sure and unfailing. Live today in light of God's love, and let compassion fill your heart with joy and steadfastness through any and every circumstance.

Extended Reading: Psalm 145

God Promises
Freedom

DEVOTIONAL

Freedom is an idea we spend most of our lives striving to experience. The bonds of slavery to the world in any fashion choke out our ability to thrive and enjoy life. We as a culture celebrate monumental events like the fall of the Berlin Wall and the global civil rights movement because we know freedom to be necessary for a life to be lived to its fullest. We fight for the freedom of those held in captivity. We advocate for those silenced by the bonds of slavery. And Scripture makes it clear that God is no different.

One of the most pervasive themes in Scripture is freedom. Its pages are filled with stories of God delivering his people from the bondage of slavery. Jesus himself freed Shadrach, Meshach, and Abednego from the fiery furnace. God shut up the mouths of lions to free Daniel. And we see God deliver the entire nation of Israel from slavery under the Egyptians through an onslaught of plagues. The Bible is clear that God works constantly to deliver his children from the yoke of slavery.

*"For freedom Christ has set us free; stand firm therefore,
and do not submit again to a yoke of slavery."*

GALATIANS 5:1

The Bible contains stories of God's deliverance from not only physical slavery but spiritual slavery as well. Romans 6:17-18 says, *"Thanks be to God, that you who were once slaves of sin have become obedient from the heart to the standard of teaching to which you were committed, and, having been set free from sin, have become slaves of righteousness."* And later Paul writes in Romans 8:1-4, *"There is therefore now no condemnation for those who are in Christ Jesus. For the law of the Spirit of life has set you free in Christ Jesus from the law of sin and death. For God has done what the law, weakened by the flesh, could not do. By sending his own Son in the likeness of sinful flesh and for sin, he condemned sin in the flesh, in order that the righteous requirement of the law might be fulfilled in us, who walk not according to the flesh but according to the Spirit."* And in Galatians 5:1, Paul writes, *"For freedom Christ has set us free; stand firm therefore, and do not submit again to a yoke of slavery."* Jesus in John 8:36 states, *"If the Son sets you free, you will be free indeed."*

Scripture is explicit that through the death and resurrection of Jesus Christ we as believers have been set free from the bondage of sin. Sin is no longer our master. The bonds to sin that entangled you to the consequences of separation from God were sacrificially broken by the blood of your Savior. You see, in the death of Jesus, God made to you his promise of freedom. He's promised that you no longer have to live life as a slave to sin. You now have available to you a life lived in the joy and power of righteousness.

God's promised you his freedom, now all that's required is for you to live in light of what God has already done for you. Cut off ties to your former life. As Paul wrote in Ephesians 4:22-24, *"Put off your old self, which belongs to your former manner of life and is corrupt through deceitful desires, and to be renewed in the spirit of your minds, and to put on the new self, created after the likeness of God in true righteousness and holiness."* Clothe yourself every day in the knowledge of who you are in Christ. Choose to live in freedom instead of sin. When you feel the tug back to your former ways, take a minute and ask the Spirit to guide you away from your former life. God's promised you his freedom. He's worked his miracle of freedom in you at salvation. You have been made new. Now live in response to God's incredible work by pursuing a life lived in righteousness. Spend time in God's presence allowing his truth and love to mold and shape you into the likeness of the very one who's saved you.

GUIDED PRAYER

1. Meditate on God's promise of your freedom from sin.

"We were buried therefore with him by baptism into death, in order that, just as Christ was raised from the dead by the glory of the Father, we too might walk in newness of life." Romans 6:4

2. Now reflect on areas of your own life in which you need to experience God's promise of freedom. Where do you feel chained to the world? What sin seems to plague you?

3. Renew your mind to the truth of what God's word says about that area. Declare the freedom Christ paid for in your life. Spend some time really thinking about God's power over your sin. Go to war with the enemy using God's truth as your weapon.

"For freedom Christ has set us free; stand firm therefore, and do not submit again to a yoke of slavery." Galatians 5:1

"So if the Son sets you free, you will be free indeed." John 8:36

"Thanks be to God, that you who were once slaves of sin have become obedient from the heart to the standard of teaching to which you were committed, and, having been set free from sin, have become slaves of righteousness." Romans 6:17-18

Follow the guidance of the Holy Spirit today as he directs you away from sin. The enemy is driven to draw you back into the sin that entangled you, but *"he who is in you is greater than he who is in the world"* (1 John 4:4). The victory is already yours. Jesus has won your freedom. The battle now is for your mind. Maintain victory over that area through the power of God's word, and the sin that seemed to be habitual will no longer have a hold over you.

Extended Reading: Romans 6–8. (These are all meant to be read together. For a full understanding read all three chapters in one sitting.)

God Promises His Comfort

DAY 12

DEVOTIONAL

2 Corinthians 1:3 tells us of a wonderful aspect of God's character, that he is *"the Father of mercies and God of all comfort."* In a world wrought with depression and hurt, we have a Father who is the source of all comfort. We serve the God of compassion and love. Let's allow the truth of God's comfort to fill us today. Let's rest in the goodness of God's presence and let him minister to any areas in which we feel hurt or depressed.

David tells us in Psalm 34:18, *"The Lord is near to the brokenhearted and saves the crushed in spirit."* Psalm 34 comes in the context of David fleeing from Saul's persecution. David, in this season of his life, knew all too well what it's like to need comfort. His circumstances were anything but peaceful. But in this moment, God faithfully delivered him again from the hands of Saul. David writes, *"This poor man cried, and the Lord heard him and saved him out of all his troubles. The angel of the Lord encamps around those who fear him, and delivers them. Oh, taste and see that the Lord is good! Blessed is the man who takes refuge in him! Oh, fear the Lord, you his saints, for those who fear him have no lack! The young lions suffer want and hunger; but those who seek the Lord lack no good thing"* (Psalm 34:6-10). David took refuge in his faithful God and found comfort. He placed his trust in the Father of all comfort and found deliverance.

It really is true that *"those who seek the Lord lack no good thing."* The same God of David is your God. You are his child. Seek him today that you might *"taste and see that the Lord is good!"* All of us are broken. All of us are hurting. All of us need the love of our heavenly Father. Where in your life today do you feel hurt? Big or small, God cares about whatever pain you might be going through. Your Father longs to heal whatever is holding you back from fullness of life in him.

Deuteronomy 33:12 says, *"The beloved of the Lord dwells in safety. The High God surrounds him all day long, and dwells between his shoulders."* You are God's beloved. You were bought at an incredible price.

He's opening up his arms to you today, asking you to simply come and find refuge from all the hurt and pain of the world in him. He desires to hold your heart today and speak his healing love over any part of you wounded by the things of the world. Spend time in his presence today allowing the Spirit of God to mend you. Allow God to cry with you, hold you, speak to you, and draw you into his process of inner healing. God's promised you his comfort, and he's always faithful to deliver on his promises. All that he asks of you is to make space in your heart for him and receive. Spend time today talking with the *"Father of all mercies and God of all comfort,"* and experience the power of being wrapped up in the powerful and loving arms of God.

GUIDED PRAYER

1. Ask God to make his nearness known to you today. Receive his presence and experience his profound, limitless peace.

"The Lord is near to all who call on him, to all who call on him in truth." Psalm 145:18

2. Open to God any part of your heart that is wounded or needs comfort. It could be the wound of a parent, spouse, friend, colleague, etc. Whatever you feel hurt by today, talk to your loving heavenly Father about it.

"The Lord is near to the brokenhearted and saves the crushed in spirit." Psalm 34:18

3. Receive God's comfort. So often healing comes simply by the compassionate love of God. As our Father, God suffers as we suffer. He hurts when we hurt. Let his nearness and love comfort you.

"Blessed be the God and Father of our Lord Jesus Christ, the Father of mercies and God of all comfort." 2 Corinthians 1:3

Healing takes time, but it is time well worth spending. We are not meant to go without the love and comfort of our heavenly Father. Seek out his presence. Spend time at length simply being loved by him. Make space for God to work and find out how willing and able he is to bind up and heal any area of your heart that feels broken.

Extended Reading: Psalm 34

God Promises His Presence

DEVOTIONAL

One of the most life-giving promises God makes to us as his children is his promise to be near. David wrote in Psalm 139:9-10, *"If I take the wings of the morning and dwell in the uttermost parts of the sea, even there your hand shall lead me, and your right hand shall hold me."* What an incredible image David paints of the nearness of God! If we were to explore the ends of the earth, God would still be there. If we were to

"If I take the wings of the morning and dwell in the uttermost parts of the sea, even there your hand shall lead me, and your right hand shall hold me."

PSALM 139:9-10

dive to the depths of the ocean, God would still be there. If we descend into the darkest places of our inner being, we will still find God. There's no place we can go that he isn't present. God's presence floods the earth like the early morning fog, saturating everything with its haze. His presence is his promise.

So, what do we do with the knowledge of God's nearness? What does it mean for us? In Deuteronomy 31:6 we're told, *"He will not leave you or forsake you."* And in Psalm 23:4 David exemplifies this command in saying, *"Even though I walk through the valley of the shadow of death, I will fear no evil, for you are with me; your rod and your staff, they comfort me."* Psalm 46:1 says it this way: *"God is our refuge and strength, a very present help in trouble."*

God's nearness is meant to be our source of courage and strength. We are to find refuge in the knowledge and experience of his presence. His presence means everything for us. It means we're not alone anymore. It means he will guide and shepherd us through the various situations we may find ourselves in: *"your rod and your staff, they comfort me."* When you wake

up in the morning, God is there to love and prepare you. When you go about your day, God is there for you, desiring to empower you. When you lay down at night, God is there to give you rest and peace. God's presence is the foundation on which so many of his other promises are fulfilled.

So if he's truly present always, why is it that we don't feel him? Why is it that we at times feel lonely, dissatisfied, weary, and weak? Encountering God's presence starts with having faith in what Scripture says. Feeling God's nearness starts with trusting that he's right next to you and wants you to know him. God doesn't force himself on us. He doesn't occupy space in our hearts that we fill with other things. So simply make space for God today, trust in his word that *"He will not leave you or forsake you,"* and encounter the nearness of your heavenly Father. Don't worry if you aren't feeling him. Your only job is to make space in your heart and trust him. He'll take care of the rest. Spend time today in prayer renewing your mind to the promise of God's presence and letting his nearness become your source of courage, strength, and rest.

69

GUIDED PRAYER

1. Meditate on the truth of God's nearness as promised in his word.

"Fear not, for I have redeemed you; I have called you by name, you are mine. When you pass through the waters, I will be with you; and through the rivers, they shall not overwhelm you; when you walk through fire you shall not be burned, and the flame shall not consume you. For I am the Lord your God, the Holy One of Israel, your Savior." Isaiah 43:1-3

2. Make space in your heart for him to fill. Trust his word. Tell him that you believe that he's right there with you. Ask the Spirit to help you make room for him to fill.

3. Now simply receive God's tangible presence. Ask him to make himself known to you. Ask him to manifest his presence to you. Remember it's really not about feeling him. Experiencing him is just the byproduct of being his child. The weight of it is all on him.

"Where shall I go from your Spirit? Or where shall I flee from your presence? If I ascend to heaven, you are there! If I make my bed in Sheol, you are there! If I take the wings of the morning and dwell in the uttermost parts of the sea, even there your hand shall lead me, and your right hand shall hold me." Psalm 139:7-10

In response to God's presence pray this prayer of Brother Lawrence to God. May his words articulate the prayer of your heart:

O my God, since thou art with me, and I must now, in obedience to thy commands, apply my mind to these outward things, I beseech thee to grant me the grace to continue in thy presence; and to this end do thou prosper me with thy assistance, receive all my works, and possess all my affections.

Extended Reading: Psalm 139

God Promises His Return

DEVOTIONAL

The second coming of Christ will mark the end of this age with resounding and final punctuation. 1 Thessalonians 4:16 says, *"For the Lord himself will descend from heaven with a cry of command, with the voice of an archangel, and with the sound of the trumpet of God."* Jesus promises that he is coming back for you and me. He's returning to make his lordship known to all the earth. Upon

"In my Father's house are many rooms. If it were not so, would I have told you that I go to prepare a place for you? And if I go and prepare a place for you, I will come again and will take you to myself, that where I am you may be also."

JOHN 14:2-3

his return, he will destroy once and for all the destructive works of the enemy. He's going to rid the earth of the damage sin has caused, and bring about the final restoration of all things to himself.

Jesus' return will be both powerful and triumphant. It will be a time of sorrow for those who did not believe in him and a time of rejoicing for us, his Bride. Jesus is coming back in all his glory, lovesick for those who have been brought into his fold by faith. You see, he's coming back for you because he loves you. He longs for the day when you can be with him, face to face, held back by nothing. He's so overjoyed to walk in relationship with you right now, but like you, he longs for something greater. Like a bridegroom patiently awaits the marriage ceremony, he's waiting, expectant for what is to come.

It's his love that is our source of hope. It's his desire for our final restoration to him that is meant to give us cause for joy here on the earth. What you've known of life thus far is not all there is. What you've experienced of God is just a drop in the vast ocean of his loving kindness. Jesus says in John 14:2-3, *"In my Father's house are many rooms. If it were not so,*

would I have told you that I go to prepare a place for you? And if I go and prepare a place for you, I will come again and will take you to myself, that where I am you may be also." He desperately wants you to be where he is. If you are a believer, he's promised that you have a place in his kingdom. You can have hope here that all the suffering, trials, temptations and heartache you've experienced on earth will pass away with his return. Written within his promise to return is his promise of a life lived free from all the destruction sin has caused.

We're meant for relationship with our Savior both here and in the age to come. He's made a way for us to experience him both now and forever by his death and resurrection. Your greatest joy should come from this truth. Your highest calling is meant to be drawn from his promise of relationship. All of eternity hinges on his promise to return. And he who gave up his life for you will return to lead you to the Father. Spend time in his presence today. Experience the very God who will return in all his glory. Live today in light of his promise, and experience the love and hope of your God who is faithful to bring to fruition all that he's promised you.

GUIDED PRAYER

1. Meditate on the powerful, hope-filled truth of Christ' return.

"In my Father's house are many rooms. If it were not so, would I have told you that I go to prepare a place for you? And if I go and prepare a place for you, I will come again and will take you to myself, that where I am you may be also." John 14:2-3

2. Where do you need hope today? Where do you need the truth of Jesus' return to transform your emotions?

3. Let the truth of Christ's return sink into your heart. Allow it to heal any place in your heart that feels hopeless.

"Let us hold fast the confession of our hope without wavering, for he who promised is faithful." Hebrews 10:23

Looking toward the day of final restoration is meant to give you fuel to live in light of eternity. This life on earth is but a vapor in the scope of your eternal life. It's a dust blowing in the wind. It doesn't mean today doesn't matter. What it does mean is that you know how your life will turn out. You know how the story ends. May the glorious, triumphant ending of your story produce steadfastness and hope in your heart today.

Extended Reading: John 14

Experiencing God's promises

"God is not man, that he should lie, or a son of man, that he should change his mind. Has he said, and will he not do it? Or has he spoken, and will he not fulfill it?" Numbers 23:19

WEEKLY OVERVIEW

Our heavenly Father has made incredible promises to us, his children. And while our God is completely faithful to deliver on his promises, he does not force them on us. He's promised his nearness, his affections, and an eternal life spent with him. But we have the power to choose our own way. He doesn't force himself where there's no space. God's word won't have power in our lives if we don't read it. We won't hear God effectively if we're not listening. And we can't experience his nearness if we constantly fill our lives with other things. So, this week we're going to talk about different ways we can experience the promises of God so that they might come to full fruition in our lives. May you encounter God powerfully as you grow in fully experiencing the incredible promises of your heavenly Father.

Waiting
on the Lord

DAY 15

DEVOTIONAL

Throughout Scripture, God gave his people the strength they needed to both sustain them through circumstances and achieve victory over their enemies. We read examples like David defeating Goliath in 1 Samuel 17, Samson defeating the Philistines in Judges 15, and Jesus crushing the power of sin and death on the cross in Matthew 27. Truly, God has promised his people his strength. But the Bible also tells us of a principle for receiving and experiencing God's strength. Isaiah 40:31 says, *"But they who wait for the Lord shall renew their strength; they shall mount up with wings like eagles; they shall run and not be weary; they shall walk and not faint."* Let's look today at the practice of waiting on God for the purpose of experiencing the strength and endurance God has promised us.

"But they who wait for the Lord shall renew their strength; they shall mount up with wings like eagles; they shall run and not be weary; they shall walk and not faint."

ISAIAH 40:31

Waiting is a practice that seems counterproductive to most of us. In a world where those who act sooner and faster seem to be more successful, the ideas of patience and waiting don't seem to have a place. But the wisdom of the world is not the wisdom of God. David was a man who was wise in the ways of experiencing God's promises. He shares with us his insight into receiving God's strength in Psalm 33:20-22: *"Our soul waits for the Lord; he is our help and our shield. For our heart is glad in him, because we trust in his holy name. Let your steadfast love, O Lord, be upon us, even as we hope in you."* God longs to shield you from the attacks of your enemy. He longs to protect you from what would tear you down. But like a shield, he can only protect you if you are willing to stay behind him. He can only help you if you are willing to be helped. You must wait on him. You must allow him to go before you and guide you.

David also gives us insight in Psalm 33 on how he was able to so effectively wait on God. He says, *"For our heart is glad in him, because we trust in his holy name."* You will only be able to wait on God to the level that you trust him. Look at your own life today. Where do

you struggle with running out in front of God? Where do you have a hard time waiting? Where do you lack patience? Trust isn't simply a matter of the head, but of the heart. To be able to actively trust God, you have to believe he truly has your best interests in mind. You have to believe in your heart that he isn't asking you to wait just to stress you out, but because he has something better for you in store.

To fully experience God's promises of strength and guidance, you must learn to trust God. You have to be willing to wait on him. God's guidance and timing are perfect. He knows how to lead you, protect you, and empower you. Trust in your heavenly Father today. Take the example David set and choose to wait on God. It's in doing so that you will experience victory. It's in waiting on the Lord that you will *"mount up with wings like eagles."* Take time today to place your trust in God. Take time to encounter his love. Let his presence fill you with the longing and ability to wait on him. And live today in response to God's word by asking for and following the guidance of the Holy Spirit in your life. He has an incredible day in store for you. Simply wait and follow wherever the Spirit leads.

GUIDED PRAYER

1. Take time to receive God's presence. Let his presence lay a foundation for you to trust him. As you experience his presence, let his goodness remind you of his character as a good Father.

2. Now think about areas of your own life where you have a hard time waiting on God. Where do you lack patience? Where do you feel scared or lacking in trust?

3. Ask the Holy Spirit to help you wait on him today. Ask him to help you trust and follow him wherever he would lead you.

"But they who wait for the Lord shall renew their strength; they shall mount up with wings like eagles; they shall run and not be weary; they shall walk and not faint."
Isaiah 40:31

Following the leading of the Spirit is about your willingness to wait and listen. And waiting and listening starts with encountering the nearness and goodness of your heavenly Father. You aren't meant to trust in a distant God. You are created to know personally the reality of your God and his love for you, and place your trust in him as a response. Wait on God today. Grow in your willingness to follow him wherever he would lead you. The Holy Spirit has the perfect way to guide you. Simply open your heart to him and listen. So great is God's love for you that he promises to go before you in every situation. He promises to be your help and shield. Stay behind your God and experience renewed strength for every circumstance you come to today.

Extended Reading: Psalm 33

Experiencing God's Promises through the Renewing of Your Mind

DAY 16

DEVOTIONAL

There is a battle being waged constantly for your mind. This battle isn't about flesh and blood, but instead about experiencing the very promises of God. You see, your mind is the place where emotions, perspectives, and decisions all collide—where lies and truth wage war. It's where you can choose to experience God and see the world as he does, or choose a different path and struggle in life to attain any sense of his promises at all. Paul writes in 2 Corinthians 10:4-5, *"For the weapons of our warfare are not of the flesh but have divine power to destroy strongholds. We destroy arguments and every lofty opinion raised against the knowledge of God, and take every thought captive to obey Christ."* Paul makes it clear that there is a very real spiritual battle happening in which taking your thoughts captive is a chief

"Do not be conformed to this world, but be transformed by the renewal of your mind, that by testing you may discern what is the will of God, what is good and acceptable and perfect."

ROMANS 12:2

weapon. So let's look today at the weapon of renewing your mind and how to effectively use it to experience all that God has in store for you.

In God we have an incredible ally in the war for our minds. We've been given the Holy Spirit to help us think like God. We've been given the word of God to meditate on so that we can share in God's wisdom. But we must engage in this process of transformation to experience all God has in store. Ephesians 4:21-24 says, *"Assuming that you have heard about him and were taught in him, as the truth is in Jesus, to put off your old self, which belongs to your former manner of life and is corrupt through deceitful desires, and to be renewed in the spirit of your minds, and to put on the new self, created after the likeness of God in true righteousness and holiness."* God has given you an opportunity for new life *"created after the very likeness of God in true righteousness and holiness."* But in order to experience that new life, you must *"be renewed in the spirit of your [mind]."* Real action is required to experience God's promise of a *"new self."* You have to see yourself as God sees you. Your perspective must shift and be aligned with God's perspective.

You see, renewing your mind positions you to fully experience God's promises. For example, Romans 12:2 says, *"Do not be conformed to this world, but be transformed by the renewal of your mind, that by testing you may discern what is the will of God, what is good and acceptable and perfect."* In the renewing of your mind, you are able to discern the will of God. It's a real and practical step to receiving the knowledge of what God would have you do. Joshua 1:8 says, *"This Book of the Law shall not depart from your mouth, but you shall meditate on it day and night, so that you may be careful to do according to all that is written in it. For then you will make your way prosperous, and then you will have good success."* In the renewing of your mind to God's word, your way will be made prosperous. Meditating on God's word has the power to lead you to success.

God's made a way for you to experience abundant life every day. He's made incredible promises to you of his will, his peace, his nearness, and his victory over the enemy. But the battle for experiencing those promises is waged in your mind. Renew your mind today to the truth of God. Take captive any lies that run through your mind. Choose to align your thinking with his word. Filter your emotions and decisions through the word of God. And experience today the abundant life God has in store for you in the goodness of his promises.

87

GUIDED PRAYER

1. Meditate for a moment on the power of renewing your mind. Allow Scripture to fill you with a desire to engage in this spiritual discipline.

"For the weapons of our warfare are not of the flesh but have divine power to destroy strongholds. We destroy arguments and every lofty opinion raised against the knowledge of God, and take every thought captive to obey Christ." 2 Corinthians 10:4-5

2. Where in your thoughts do you need victory today? Where do you feel like your perspective of yourself, others, or situations might not align with God's perspective?

3. Renew your mind to God's truth in those areas. Find Scripture that speaks to those areas. Ask the Spirit to guide you in renewing your mind to the truth you need.

You can take inventory of the battle being waged for your mind by simply looking at your life. Look at your emotions. Look at the decisions you're making. You have the power to control those areas of your life by renewing your mind. God's word is unchanging. His perspective is sure, steadfast, and perfect. He's given you the tools you need to align your thinking with his in his Spirit and his word. Choose to engage in the life-giving process of renewing your mind. If you'll choose to act on God's word, to believe him, your heart will become steadfast and unshakable. You'll experience a life full of the abundance of God's promises. May your day be filled with the promises of God fulfilled in your life.

Extended Reading: 2 Corinthians 10

Live for His Glory

DEVOTIONAL

One of the most constant and critical struggles we as believers have is balancing our God-given longing for greatness with striving for our own glory on earth. You were made to long for greatness. You were made to do earth-shattering, bondage-breaking, life-giving works. But the Bible makes it clear that when we overstep the boundary of greatness to glory we step outside of the abundant life God desires to give us. When we long to achieve greatness for our own fame and reputation, we load onto our shoulders a weight only God can bear. Living for your own glory will only lead you to a life of dissatisfaction, striving, burdens, and failure. So, let's take some time today and cast the burden of achieving glory back onto the only person who deserves it and can bear it, our Savior King, Jesus Christ.

Philippians 2:9-11 says, *"Therefore God has highly exalted him and bestowed on him the name that is above every name, so that at the name of Jesus every knee should bow, in heaven and on earth and under the earth, and every tongue confess that Jesus Christ is Lord, to the glory of God the Father."* Our Lord, Jesus Christ, is the exalted One. He alone is the One True King. All of creation is under his rule and authority. God alone can bear the burden of glory. With glory comes great responsibility—responsibility you and I will never be able to bear. In Isaiah 42:8 God says, *"I am the Lord; that is my name; my glory I give to no other, nor my praise to carved idols."* Romans 11:36 says, *"For from him and through him and to him are all things. To him be glory forever. Amen."* Jesus doesn't want glory because he's prideful or selfish. He is lifted up because he is the way to the Father. He's not looking for control of our lives for selfish gain. He knows that when he takes the throne of our hearts, he can lead us into abundant life. Through Jesus we have restored relationship with our heavenly Father. Through Jesus our sins have been blotted out. You and I have been made clean in the sight of God. And we will live in eternal communion with God himself all by Jesus' death and resurrection. It's in living for his glory that we will find peace and purpose. And it's only in living for his glory that the world will come to know the Father.

So, what does it look like to live for the glory of God? Living for God's glory requires true humility. Humility isn't acting as if you're bad at things you are good at. You don't have to turn away every kind or encouraging word that gets spoken to you. True humility is acknowledging God has given you the gifts and talents you possess and acting on that knowledge by living for God's glory alone. True humility takes compliments and encouragement straight to God in the secret place, laying down any good thing you've done back at the feet of Jesus in worship. Again, you are meant for greatness. You are designed to live a life of effective and good work. Just don't take credit where credit is not due.

How can you lead a life devoted to the glory of God? You must first begin by spending time encountering the glory of God for yourself. Psalm 97:1-5 says, *"The Lord reigns, let the earth rejoice; let the many coastlands be glad! Clouds and thick darkness are all around him; righteousness and justice are the foundation of his throne. Fire goes before him and burns up his adversaries all around. His lightnings light up the world; the earth sees and trembles. The mountains melt like wax before the Lord, before the Lord of all the earth."*

God's glory is here on the earth. All throughout Scripture we read of God's glory displayed throughout creation. His glory is revealed in his love, in his nearness, and even in you as God's crown of creation. Spend time meditating on how glorious God is. Spend time worshipping your King. When you encounter the glory of God consistently, your desires will naturally shift from living for yourself to living for him. Second, align your purposes with God's purposes. Pursue relationships, work, fun, and community in light of your need to live for God's glory. And lastly, spend time in God's presence allowing the Spirit to mold and shape you. Make room for God to align your desires with his. Ask for the Spirit's help every day as you work and play. Open yourself to his leading as he helps you pursue a life lived for the glory of God. God has a plan every day to use you for his kingdom. He has so many promises he longs for you to experience all day. Live for the glory of God and experience the abundant peace and joy he has planned for you.

GUIDED PRAYER

1. Spend time meditating on the glory of God. Think about all of the marvelous works he has done.

"The Lord reigns, let the earth rejoice; let the many coastlands be glad! Clouds and thick darkness are all around him; righteousness and justice are the foundation of his throne. Fire goes before him and burns up his adversaries all around. His lightnings light up the world; the earth sees and trembles. The mountains melt like wax before the Lord, before the Lord of all the earth."
Psalm 97:1–5

2. Reflect on areas in your own life where you struggle with pride and living for your own glory.

3. Now ask the Holy Spirit to help you live for God's glory in those areas where you struggle. Ask him to show you what it looks like to live for the glory of Jesus today. Choose to respond to his leadership with obedience and faith.

"So, whether you eat or drink, or whatever you do, do all to the glory of God." 1 Corinthians 10:31

"Blessed be his glorious name forever; may the whole earth be filled with his glory! Amen and Amen!" Psalm 72:19

Living for God's glory is a process. It is a lifestyle radically different than any other way of living. It requires continual humbling and repentance. Know that God has total grace for you today. He knows what is holding you back from fully encountering him. He knows what entangles you to the ways of the world. And he has a perfect plan to deliver you from any bondage that you may be experiencing. Trust him and have patience. Come before his throne as often as possible, and lay down your achievements at his feet. Experience the glory of God through his love and creation. Let his loving kindness mold and shape you into the likeness of Jesus. Live for the glory of God today and experience a life free from the burden of pursuing fame and reputation.

Extended Reading: Psalm 97

Trust in
God's Promise

DEVOTIONAL

The Bible consistently gives us an image to visualize when thinking about the character of God. Psalm 18:2 says, *"The Lord is my rock and my fortress and my deliverer, my God, my rock, in whom I take refuge, my shield, and the horn of my salvation, my stronghold."* 2 Samuel 22:32 says, *"For who is God, but the Lord? And who is a rock, except our God?"* I love how the

"You keep him in perfect peace whose mind is stayed on you, because he trusts in you. Trust in the Lord forever, for the Lord God is an everlasting rock."

ISAIAH 26:3-4

Lord chooses to use creation to tell us of the invisible attributes of his nature. To our eyes, rocks are unchanging, steady, and stable. Generations of men come and go, but rocks stay visually the same. So it is with our God. 1 Kings 8:56 says, *"Blessed be the Lord who has given rest to his people Israel, according to all that he promised. Not one word has failed of all his good promise, which he spoke by Moses his servant."* The promises of God are sure. They are even more immovable than the strongest mountains. They are more steadfast than the very ground you walk on.

You can place your trust in God and believe he'll follow through on his promises. In fact, experiencing his promises to the extent God intends for you requires trust. Isaiah 26:3-4 says, *"You keep him in perfect peace whose mind is stayed on you, because he trusts in you. Trust in the Lord forever, for the Lord God is an everlasting rock."* Throughout Scripture, God leads his people to peace. He's promised peace to us as his children. But Isaiah 26 tells us of an incredibly important concept. Those who will be kept in *"perfect peace"* are those *"whose mind is stayed"* on God. And a mind can only be stayed on God *"because he trusts in [him]."*

Experiencing the fullness of God's promises requires our steadfast trust. For example, Philippians 4:19 says, *"My God will supply every need of yours according to his riches in glory in Christ Jesus."* God promises to *"supply every need of yours."* His promise is sure. But experiencing the peace his promise of provision is meant to supply requires trusting in his word. He will provide for your needs regardless of your trust, but you won't be able to experience the peace God longs to give if you're constantly worried about whether or not you'll be provided for. The commonly quoted promise of Jeremiah 29:11 says, *"For I know the plans I have for you, declares the Lord, plans for welfare and not for evil, to give you a future and a hope."* God will still have an incredible plan for your life regardless of whether you trust his word. But God's promise is meant to produce in you an unshakable assurance. You are created to live your life trusting that God has a plan for you and will reveal it to you perfectly. Experiencing that assurance requires the act of trusting God's character and leadership.

Where do you need *"perfect peace"* today? Where do you need rest for your soul? Search out the promises of God. Remember that his promises are sure. He is your rock and your refuge. Place your trust in his promises as often as it takes until they produce peace in your life. Choose continually to place your hope in God and live a life of faith in response to his faithfulness. God has a plan to lead you to peace today. He has a plan to produce joy and hope in you that can't be taken away by any circumstance or fear. Experience all that God's promises are meant to produce today by trusting in your Rock, your everlasting and loving heavenly Father.

GUIDED PRAYER

1. Meditate on God's immovable promises.

"The Lord is my rock and my fortress and my deliverer, my God, my rock, in whom I take refuge, my shield, and the horn of my salvation, my stronghold." Psalm 18:2

2. Where in your life do you need to experience more of the fruit of God's promises? Where do you need peace and hope?

3. Choose to place your trust in God today. Search out his promises that have to do with areas in your life that cause you worry or fear, and then place your trust in those promises.

"You keep him in perfect peace whose mind is stayed on you, because he trusts in you. Trust in the Lord forever, for the Lord God is an everlasting rock." Isaiah 26:3-4

The Lord has incredible patience to lead you through the process of trusting him. God knows that experiencing all that the Christian life is intended to give requires incredible faith. Jesus said, *"Blessed are those who have not seen and yet have believed"* (John 20:29). If you find yourself fearful, worried, our doubting, it is all right. Just don't stay there! Search out God's promises. Spend time in prayer. Spend time *"casting all your anxieties on him, because he cares for you"* (1 Peter 5:7). Trusting God is a lifelong pursuit. But it is a pursuit worth all of your time and energy. Commit yourself to spending time exploring and experiencing the faithfulness of God. Let his steadfast love produce in you trust and hope. Place your trust today in your God, the only one who will never fail you.

Extended Reading: Isaiah 26

97

Casting Off Negativity

DEVOTIONAL

Negativity is like a weed that robs us of the vitality available in thankfulness, in right thinking, and in saying only that which builds up. Negativity never serves to edify, produce life, or lead to anything positive. It can serve only the purpose of destruction. Let's spend time today looking at what the Bible says about negativity, learning how we can stop its destruction, and ask the Holy Spirit to be our Helper in ridding it from our lives. Scripture speaks very harshly of the power of an unbridled tongue. James 3:2-6 says:

For we all stumble in many ways. And if anyone does not stumble in what he says, he is a perfect man, able also to bridle his whole body. If we put bits into the mouths of horses so that they obey us, we guide their whole bodies as well. Look at the ships also: though they are so large and are driven by strong winds, they are guided by a very small rudder wherever the will of the pilot directs. So also the tongue is a small member, yet it boasts of great things. How great a forest is set ablaze by such a small fire! And the tongue is a fire, a world of unrighteousness. The tongue is set among our members, staining the whole body, setting on fire the entire course of life, and set on fire by hell.

The tongue is the rudder that leads to a life of *"unrighteousness"* or a life lived in honor and obedience to God. Proverbs 18:21 says, *"Death and life are in the power of the tongue, and those who love it will eat its fruits."* Speaking negatively produces the fruit of unrighteousness while speaking words of thankfulness and grace produces life. Proverbs 26:20 says, *"For lack of wood the fire goes out, and where there is no whisperer, quarreling ceases."* We've all experienced the harmful effects of slander. If we will choose to cut out negativity, we can put out the destructive fire slander causes. Finally, Proverbs 15:4 says, *"A gentle tongue is a tree of life, but perverseness in it breaks the spirit."*

Have you experienced the power of negativity in your own life? How does speaking negatively about a person affect your feelings toward them? How

> *"Death and life are in the power of the tongue, and those who love it will eat its fruits."*

PROVERBS 18:21

does speaking negatively of a situation affect your perspective for the day? Now think about the opposite. What does it do for your emotions and perspectives to speak positively? How do you feel when you express thankfulness about your life instead of negativity? As we learned in Proverbs 15:4, *"A gentle tongue is a tree of life."* When you speak gently of others you will find life produced not only in yourself but in them as well. When you co-labor with God's heart in sharing his message of love, grace, and peace, the result is a wellspring of life.

Negativity is not the same as correcting those around you face-to-face. The Bible speaks highly of correction motivated by love. And we need people around us that have the courage and love to correct us when we're wrong. However, there is no place for negativity in the lives of believers. You don't need it! You don't have to speak negatively about people and situations. You can always choose to speak thankfulness, grace, and love. Think for a minute about what your life would look like without negativity. How would your attitudes, emotions, and perspective be different? Would you enjoy your life more? Would others enjoy you more?

The Holy Spirit is here to help you express thankfulness instead of negativity. He is always looking for opportunities to lead you into a life more full of the abundance and enjoyment of God's righteousness. He is faithful to guide you into a fruitful life lived in obedience to him. God will never give you a command he won't help you obey. He is not a God who sits back firing rules at his people from afar. He is a God who comes down off his throne to die in order to make a way for you to live a better life full of restored relationship with him. Choose thankfulness today over negativity and rid yourself of that which robs you of experiencing God's promise of abundant life. Spend time with him today in his presence, let his love and grace stir up thankfulness within you, and receive the help that comes from the Holy Spirit's guidance in your life.

GUIDED PRAYER

1. Meditate on what God says about the power of your speech.

"Death and life are in the power of the tongue, and those who love it will eat its fruits." Proverbs 18:21

"It is not what goes into the mouth that defiles a person, but what comes out of the mouth; this defiles a person." Matthew 15:11

2. Now reflect on people and situations that seem to constantly produce negativity in your life. Where do you most often feel anger, frustration, and negativity? Who consistently leads you to speak negatively about people or situations?

3. Ask the Holy Spirit to help you speak life and thankfulness today instead of negativity. Think back on those people and circumstances. Focus on what you can be thankful for today. Thank God for what he is doing in those people and circumstances that seem to consistently produce negativity in you.

When you begin to notice yourself speaking negatively today, stop and ask the Holy Spirit to guide you into an attitude of thankfulness. Hold captive your thoughts today. Catch them before you speak them. Choose to speak life into people around you. Spread God's love today. And watch as your day is transformed into being more joyful, peaceful, and full of life.

Extended Reading: James 3

Make Time to Experience God

DAY 20

DEVOTIONAL

Our world deems the busiest people to be the most successful. We look at the lives of those who work more than the average person and admire their fortitude and drive. We compare our own lives to those who seem to work more, have more, and do more with their time and wish we could have the resolve to be more like them. As a result of society's epidemic of busyness, our spiritual lives are suffering. The Bible gives us a clear depiction of the life of a busy person and the life of a person who made time to sit and experience God. Luke 10:38-42 says,

Now as they went on their way, Jesus entered a village. And a woman named Martha welcomed him into her house. And she had a sister called Mary, who sat at the Lord's feet and listened to his teaching. But Martha was distracted with much serving. And she went up to him and said, "Lord, do you not care that my sister has left me to serve alone? Tell her then to help me." But the Lord answered her, "Martha, Martha, you are anxious and troubled about many things, but one thing is necessary. Mary has chosen the good portion, which will not be taken away from her."

Jesus' response in the last two sentences strikes me to the core. Jesus says, *"Martha, Martha, you are anxious and troubled about many things, but one thing is necessary. Mary has chosen the good portion, which will not be taken away from her."* The good portion in Jesus' eyes was to sit and listen to him, an idea that contradicts most of what we value in our culture. We value those who fill their time with service and action. But that's not what Jesus valued. Jesus valued Mary, who spent her time sitting at his feet. Jesus valued Mary's willingness to make time to be with him. And we don't just find this teaching in this one instance either! Psalm 127:2 says, *"It is in vain that you rise up early and go late to rest, eating the bread of anxious toil; for he gives to his beloved sleep."* Psalm 37:7 says, *"Be still before the Lord and wait patiently*

"Be still before the Lord and wait patiently for him;
fret not yourself over the one who prospers in his
way, over the man who carries out evil devices!"

PSALM 37:7

for him; fret not yourself over the one who prospers in
his way, over the man who carries out evil devices!"
Clearly there is a principle of rest and making space
for God that spans across the entirety of Scripture.

So, how can we respond to God's word today?
What does this principle of making time to spend
with God mean for us? First, we have to choose to
value God's word over the opinion of man. Martha
was angry with Mary. Martha must have felt that
Mary was lazy and selfish the way many of us
would. But Scripture is clear that Martha was wrong.
Will you value God's opinion over man's? Will you
choose to rest in God's presence when the world
is knocking at your door, telling you to get busy?

Second, we have to re-evaluate what we call
success. Busyness and monetary gain aren't the
definition of success in God's eyes. Working
tirelessly, even for his kingdom, isn't the same as

working with God. We have to make room in our
lives to experience God and his promises. God can't
bring you peace and a deeper revelation of his love
if you don't make time to encounter him. Martha
proved this concept. She was in the very presence
of the living God and only experienced anxiety and
frustration. You have to make time to sit at the feet
of Jesus with no agenda. Simply being with God is
foundational to living the Christian life. Isaiah 30:15
says, *"For thus said the Lord God, the Holy One of*
Israel, 'In returning and rest you shall be saved; in
quietness and in trust shall be your strength.' But you
were unwilling." You must be willing to rest. You have
to make time for God's presence. He's waiting right
now to restore you and fill you with peace. He has
a perfect plan to satisfy the longings of your heart.
Wait on God today. Wait for the leading of his Holy
Spirit. Receive the love and affection God is longing
to give, and let it be the fuel that spurs you toward
good works today.

GUIDED PRAYER

1. Meditate on the story of Mary and Martha. Place yourself in Scripture. Let the truth of Jesus' words shift your perspective on success.

"Now as they went on their way, Jesus entered a village. And a woman named Martha welcomed him into her house. And she had a sister called Mary, who sat at the Lord's feet and listened to his teaching. But Martha was distracted with much serving. And she went up to him and said, 'Lord, do you not care that my sister has left me to serve alone? Tell her then to help me.' But the Lord answered her, 'Martha, Martha, you are anxious and troubled about many things, but one thing is necessary. Mary has chosen the good portion, which will not be taken away from her.'" Luke 10:38-42

2. Now reflect on your own life. Are you too busy? What perspective, person, or fear drives you to busyness?

3. Ask God to guide you into a life of consistently making time to experience him. Ask the Holy Spirit to show you what needs to change in your life. What do you need to get rid of or say no to? Hand over whatever is holding you back from your heavenly Father in prayer. Cast all your burdens on his shoulders and find rest in his love.

Let encountering God be your fuel for action today. Move as he moves. Wait when he calls you to wait. Surrender your day to the Holy Spirit and follow his guidance. There are whole days God is calling you to simply rest in his presence. Decide to value God's opinion over man's today and spend time resting in the presence of your heavenly Father. There will be a time and place to work, seeing his kingdom come to earth, but he will faithfully lead you to those moments. Choose to wait on God today, rest in his presence, and experience a new strength for your day that can only be found in sitting at the feet of Jesus.

Extended Reading: Isaiah 30

Be the Hands
and Feet of Jesus

DAY 21

DEVOTIONAL

One of the best ways to experience the promises of God is to co-labor with him in his purposes of restoration. It's incredible that God's plan is to use us, his church, to see his kingdom come to earth. He's commissioned us to spread the gospel. He's chosen us to tell of the good news of restored relationship with our Creator.

Matthew 28:16-20 says, *"Now the eleven disciples went to Galilee, to the mountain to which Jesus had directed them. And when they saw him they worshiped him, but some doubted. And Jesus came and said to them, 'All authority in heaven and on earth has been given to me. Go therefore and make disciples of all nations, baptizing them in the name of the Father and of the Son and of the Holy Spirit, teaching them to observe all that I have commanded you. And behold, I am with you always, to the end of the age.'"* Jesus shares with us the authority that's been given to him. God's made incredible promises to his people, and he wants us to join him in seeing his promises come to fruition.

"All this is from God, who through Christ reconciled us to himself and gave us the ministry of reconciliation; that is, in Christ God was reconciling the world to himself, not counting their trespasses against them, and entrusting to us the message of reconciliation."

2 CORINTHIANS 5:18-19

We get to share with the world a message like Peter's in Acts 2:38, *"Repent and be baptized every one of you in the name of Jesus Christ for the forgiveness of your sins, and you will receive the gift of the Holy Spirit,"* and bring to fruition the promise of Jesus that *"God so loved the world, that he gave his only Son, that whoever believes in him should not perish but have eternal life. For God did not send his Son into the world to condemn the world, but in order that the world might be saved through him"* (John 3:16-17). How incredible! You have the opportunity to see God's promise of salvation come to those around you through working with God!

You can also co-labor with God in his desire to meet the felt needs of those around you. God says in Deuteronomy 15:11, *"There will never cease to be poor in the land. Therefore I command you, 'You shall open wide your hand to your brother, to the needy and to the poor, in your land.'"* The church in Acts brought about God's desire to meet needs. Acts 4:34-35 says, *"There was not a needy person among them, for as many as were owners of lands or houses sold them and brought the proceeds of what was sold and laid it at the apostles' feet, and it was distributed*

to each as any had need." God longs to use you like he did his church in Acts. You get to work with God in seeing his longing to provide for people come to pass. You get to be the hands and feet of our Savior and co-labor with Christ.

2 Corinthians 5:18-19 says, *"All this is from God, who through Christ reconciled us to himself and gave us the ministry of reconciliation; that is, in Christ God was reconciling the world to himself, not counting their trespasses against them, and entrusting to us the message of reconciliation."* As the child of God, you've been set apart for the works of your Father. You've been entrusted with the incredible *"message of reconciliation."* There is no other work in life that will fill you with more joy and purpose than seeing God's promises fulfilled through your own hands. What an incredible God we have, that in all his power and wisdom he would choose to use us as his hands and feet. Your God loves you and empowers you for incredible works that will satisfy the desires of your heart and the needs of others. Spend time in his presence today being fueled by his love. Follow the leading of the Spirit as he shows you where he is working and what he would have you do to see his promises come to fruition through your life.

107

GUIDED PRAYER

1. Meditate on God's desire to use you to bring about his message of reconciliation.

"All this is from God, who through Christ reconciled us to himself and gave us the ministry of reconciliation; that is, in Christ God was reconciling the world to himself, not counting their trespasses against them, and entrusting to us the message of reconciliation." 2 Corinthians 5:18-19

2. Ask the Spirit to show you where and how he would have you minister today. Who do you know that needs God's love today? What can you do to see God's promises come to pass in the lives of others?

"There was not a needy person among them, for as many as were owners of lands or houses sold them and brought the proceeds of what was sold and laid it at the apostles' feet, and it was distributed to each as any had need." Acts 4:34-35

3. Commit yourself to do what the Lord shows you. Ask the Holy Spirit to empower you to accomplish the works he's set before you. Receive his presence and let God's love fuel you toward all that he has in store for you.

God's intention is not to burden you with the work he's set before you. His intention is actually to lead you to a better and more fulfilling life. He knows that you will only be truly satisfied when you partner with him to see his kingdom come to earth. You are meant for good works. You are meant to co-labor with your heavenly Father. Any time you feel burdened, simply cast your cares on God. Ask him to share his heart with you. Minister from his anointing and not your own strength. May you find today a lifestyle of good works that leads you to joy, peace, and purpose in the Spirit.

Extended Reading: 2 Corinthians 5

Knowing the heart of God

"Now this is eternal life: that they know you, the only true God, and Jesus Christ, whom you have sent."
John 17:3

WEEKLY OVERVIEW

One of the greatest privileges as a child of God is that we can have the heart of our heavenly Father. We don't have to wonder how he feels about us. We don't have to wonder if he will guide us. We don't have to question whether he loves us or cares about us. Through the Holy Spirit we have continual, free access to the heart of God. May your relationship with God go deeper and become freer as you build trust and learn how to have God's heart this week.

You Can Know God

DEVOTIONAL

God longs to be known by you. He longs for you to make time to simply seek his face and get to know his personality, the nature of his love, and the availability of his presence. You don't have to live without a real, revelatory knowledge of God's heart. You don't have to live with the uncertainty of whether you are cared for, provided for, and loved.

*"Be still, and know that I am God; I will be exalted
among the nations, I will be exalted in the earth."*

PSALM 46:10

117

In the life, death, and resurrection of Jesus, God proved his longing to be known by us. Jesus took on flesh not just so he could save and redeem us, but so he could usher in a better, truer revelation of who the Father is. In John 17:3 Jesus says, *"Now this is eternal life: that they know you, the only true God, and Jesus Christ, whom you have sent."* And later in verse 26 Jesus prays to the Father, *"I have made you known to them, and will continue to make you known in order that the love you have for me may be in them and that I myself may be in them."* Jesus came that we might know the love of the Father. He came that we might have communion—unhindered relationship with our Creator.

Through Jesus you've been granted eternal, real access to your heavenly Father. And in the Holy Spirit you can search the deep places of God's heart and grow in restored relationship with him. 1 Corinthians 2:10-12 says:

For the Spirit searches everything, even the depths of God. For who knows a person's thoughts except the spirit of that person, which is in him? So also no one comprehends the thoughts of God except the Spirit of God. Now we have received not the spirit of the world, but the Spirit who is from God, that we might understand the things freely given us by God.

God has made the way for you to know his heart. You can know him in infinitely deeper and more transformative ways than you can know even your best friend or spouse. The Holy Spirit, God himself, dwells within you and longs to reveal the *"deep things of God"* to you.

All that's left for you to do is have faith in God's ability to reveal himself when you seek him and set aside time to know the heart of your heavenly Father. May you make time to do exactly that today as you enter into guided prayer.

GUIDED PRAYER

1. Meditate on what Scripture says about the knowability of God's heart. Let God's word fill you with faith to seek deeper relationship with your Father.

"For the Spirit searches everything, even the depths of God. For who knows a person's thoughts except the spirit of that person, which is in him? So also no one comprehends the thoughts of God except the Spirit of God. Now we have received not the spirit of the world, but the Spirit who is from God, that we might understand the things freely given us by God." 1 Corinthians 2:10-12

"Now this is eternal life: that they know you, the only true God, and Jesus Christ, whom you have sent." John 17:3

"I have made you known to them, and will continue to make you known in order that the love you have for me may be in them and that I myself may be in them." John 17:26

2. Ask God to reveal an aspect of his heart that you need to know. Ask him how he feels about you in this moment. Ask him to reveal just how near and loving he is. Rest in his presence.

3. Thank God for how available he is to you. Worship him because he's paid the ultimate price simply for you to know him. As you pour out thankfulness on him, watch as he pours his presence out over you.

What a tragedy it is to not take full advantage of what Jesus paid so high a price to accomplish. What a waste to live this life as if God isn't fully with us, fully for us, and fully available to us. He couldn't make the way to his heart any clearer. The Holy Spirit dwells within you as close to your heart as he could possibly be. Knowing God is as simple as acknowledging how close and available he already is. May your life be changed in light of the knowability of your perfect, loving heavenly Father.

Extended Reading: John 17

Continual Revelation

DEVOTIONAL

Seeking God isn't meant to be a one-time event. We're not meant to run off the fuel of an occasional encounter with our Father's love. Rather, seeking and finding God's heart is to be at the foundation of all we do. It's to be intertwined in our thoughts, actions, and emotions. He longs to reveal himself to us whether we're at home, working, watching movies, in a church service, or out with friends. Life with God is meant to be about continual revelation of his heart.

In Jeremiah 29:13-14 God says, *"You will seek me and find me, when you seek me with all your heart. I will be found by you, declares the Lord."* God longs to be found by us. He longs for us to seek out a revelation of his invisible nature, unconditional love, and abounding grace. He longs for us to taste and see that he is good (Psalm 34:8). When you seek out God you won't be met with nothingness. When you seek to know the will, attributes, feelings, and reality of your heavenly Father, you will find what you seek. His presence is his promise.

I go through too much of my day apart from a revelation of God's heart. I suffer through insecurities, disappointments, fear, doubt, and worry as if I am on my own. I take my life into my own hands and work to feel valued, fight for what I feel is owed me, feel like quitting when I fail, and wallow in my inability to live life perfectly, when all the while my heavenly Father waits, beckoning me with his grace to simply ask him for his heart. All the while he longs to root and ground me in his love that isn't based on what I do, but based on his unwavering, unchanging character.

The best news we have today is that God is available to us. He's ready and willing to pour out a love so rich, so real, and so powerful that everything changes. He's knocking on the door of our hearts, hoping that we will simply take the time to open up and let him in. Take time today as we enter into guided pray to seek a fresh revelation of God's heart. Begin a lifestyle of continually seeking God by giving God all you have right now: yourself. May you be empowered and set free today to live in communion with your loving heavenly Father.

GUIDED PRAYER

1. Reflect on the importance of continually seeking God that he might be continually found.

"You will seek me and find me, when you seek me with all your heart. I will be found by you, declares the Lord."
Jeremiah 29:13-14

"Seek the Lord and his strength; seek his presence continually!"
1 Chronicles 16:11

2. Ask God for a fresh revelation of his heart today. Take time to quiet yourself and open your heart to receive.

3. Spend some time in solitude simply being with God. Rather than asking him questions, journal what you are discovering about God. Write down how you feel, aspects of his character you are noticing, and what he seems to be speaking to you.

"Be still, and know that I am God." Psalm 46:10

Sometimes simply being with God teaches us more than a thousand questions he could answer. In being still and knowing he is God we learn the reality of his presence and the communion we have with him. We discover his personality and learn to trust in his quiet, calm assurance. There's nothing as comforting as sitting with him and simply knowing that he has us. May you find peace and comfort in the nearness of God today.

Extended Reading: Psalm 46

The Word

DEVOTIONAL

Scripture is one of the best indications we have of God's intense longing to be known by his people. Every time we open up the Bible we are looking at a miracle. God has revealed himself to us in a way that is beyond dispute and beyond anything we could ask or imagine. Within the pages of Scripture

> *"For the word of God is living and active, sharper
> than any two-edged sword, piercing to the division of
> soul and of spirit, of joints and of marrow, and
> discerning the thoughts and intentions of the heart."*

HEBREWS 4:12

we see countless examples of God's grace, love, presence, power, and unfathomable desire to have a restored relationship with us.

Oftentimes I take for granted how amazing it is to have the Bible. Because I grew up knowing Scripture to be God's word, it was always normal to me. Never before had I looked at it and realized what a powerful declaration it was of God's desire to be known by me. And our Father didn't just leave us with some words he spoke thousands of years ago, but gave us the Holy Spirit to help us understand and receive revelation from the word.

In reading Scripture with the Holy Spirit we can come to a real, transformative understanding of God's heart. There is no refuting what God says in the Bible. There is no questioning whether the words we're reading are true, important, or applicable.

Hebrews 4:12 says, *"For the word of God is living and active, sharper than any two-edged sword, piercing to the division of soul and of spirit, of joints and of marrow, and discerning the thoughts and intentions of the heart."* 2 Timothy 3:16 says, *"All Scripture is breathed out by God and profitable for teaching, for reproof, for correction, and for training in righteousness."* And Romans 15:4 says, *"For whatever was written in former days was written for our instruction, that through endurance and through the encouragement of the Scriptures we might have hope."*

If you're longing to know the heart of God today, search his word. God has preserved the Bible you have today for the purpose of revealing himself. When you seek him out through the reading of Scripture with the help of the Holy Spirit, you will find him. May your time of guided prayer be filled with revelation and transformation as God's heart is revealed.

GUIDED PRAYER

1. Meditate on the power of Scripture in revealing God's heart.

"For the word of God is living and active, sharper than any two-edged sword, piercing to the division of soul and of spirit, of joints and of marrow, and discerning the thoughts and intentions of the heart." Hebrews 4:12

"My son, be attentive to my words; incline your ear to my sayings. Let them not escape from your sight; keep them within your heart. For they are life to those who find them, and healing to all their flesh. Keep your heart with all vigilance, for from it flow the springs of life." Proverbs 4:20-23

2. Ask the Holy Spirit to reveal the heart of God as you read his word. Have faith that God longs to reveal himself to you.

3. Take time to read Scripture. Pick a passage of Scripture and write down aspects of God's heart you find. Place your hope and trust in the words of the Bible.

"Your words were found, and I ate them, and your words became to me a joy and the delight of my heart, for I am called by your name, O Lord, God of hosts." Jeremiah 15:16

Reading Scripture with the Holy Spirit brings God's word to life. The Bible isn't just a book of rules. It's not just a list of do's and don'ts. It's meant to be read with the understanding that its words were inspired by the One who dwells within you. May your heart be stirred to meditate on God's word that it might produce peace and joy in your life today.

Extended Reading: Joshua 1

The Spirit

DEVOTIONAL

The Holy Spirit dwelling inside of us as believers is our gateway to the heart of God. It's through him that we can know the thoughts, emotions, and will of the Father. It's through him that we grow in our revelation of God through Scripture. And it's through him that we encounter God's manifest presence.

"When the Spirit of truth comes, he will guide you into all the truth, for he will not speak on his own authority, but whatever he hears he will speak, and he will declare to you the things that are to come."

JOHN 16:13

In John 16:13 Jesus says, *"When the Spirit of truth comes, he will guide you into all the truth, for he will not speak on his own authority, but whatever he hears he will speak, and he will declare to you the things that are to come."* 1 Corinthians 2:10-11 says, *"The Spirit searches everything, even the depths of God. For who knows a person's thoughts except the spirit of that person, which is in him? So also no one comprehends the thoughts of God except the Spirit of God."*

Encountering the heart of God through the Holy Spirit is meant to be normal for believers. It's not supposed to be weird to hear from God. It's not only for the chosen few to know God's heart moment to moment. We're created to know the Father and the Son by the Holy Spirit. We're created for real, authentic, and transformative relationship with the entire Godhead.

Unless we allow God to create a new normal for us, we will never experience the fullness of life Jesus died to give us. Unless we open our hearts to the Spirit and allow him to teach us how to live life in communion with him, we will never be rooted and grounded in God's love and grace. And without being rooted in the love of God the storms of this life will always wreak unnecessary havoc.

The Spirit longs to lead you to the heart of God today. He longs to share with you the *"thoughts of God."* He longs for you to know the depths of his love and grace. Allow God to create a new normal for you today. Seek out his will before decisions you are unsure of. Seek out his heart when you feel distraught, insecure, or frustrated. And seek out his manifest presence when the cares of the world begin to weigh on you. May you grow in fellowship with the Spirit who dwells within you as you enter into a time of guided prayer.

GUIDED PRAYER

1. Meditate on the availability of knowing God's heart through the Holy Spirit. Allow Scripture to fill you with a desire for a new normal.

"When the Spirit of truth comes, he will guide you into all the truth, for he will not speak on his own authority, but whatever he hears he will speak, and he will declare to you the things that are to come." John 16:13

"The Spirit searches everything, even the depths of God. For who knows a person's thoughts except the spirit of that person, which is in him? So also no one comprehends the thoughts of God except the Spirit of God." 1 Corinthians 2:10-11

2. How connected are you with God moment to moment? Are you living with a continual awareness of his heart? Journal an honest assessment of your relationship.

3. Ask the Holy Spirit to lead you into a lifestyle of deeper, more continuous encounters with the heart of God. Decide today that you don't want to live apart from an awareness of God's will, love, and nearness.

In Exodus 33:14 God says, *"My presence will go with you, and I will give you rest."* God will go with you today. There is nowhere you could go that he won't be ready to love you and reveal himself to you. You've been granted wonderful, supernatural access to the heart of God through the life, death, and resurrection of Jesus. May you find rest in the presence of the living God today.

Extended Reading: 1 Corinthians 2

Revelation
through Others

DEVOTIONAL

One of the chief ways God reveals his heart to us is revelation through fellow believers. Hebrews 10:24-25 says, *"And let us consider how to stir up one another to love and good works, not neglecting to meet together, as is the habit of some, but encouraging one another, and all the more as you see the Day drawing near."* God has given us the ability to encourage one another—to literally fill the hearts of fellow believers with courage to pursue fullness of life in the kingdom. He's given us the ability to *"stir up one another to love and good works"* that we might fill one another with wholehearted devotion to Jesus both in word and deed.

One of my favorite passages of Scripture is 2 Corinthians 4:5-7. Paul writes:

For what we proclaim is not ourselves, but Jesus Christ as Lord, with ourselves as your servants for Jesus' sake. For God, who said, 'Let light shine out of darkness,' has shone in our hearts to give the light of the knowledge of the glory of God in the face of Jesus Christ. But we have this treasure in jars of clay, to show that the surpassing power belongs to God and not to us.

God has given us his glory. He's given us the ability to proclaim not only ourselves, but *"Jesus Christ as Lord."* The jars of clay Paul was referencing here were anything but perfect. They were fragile and easily broken. They were the material for the common person.

God has chosen to display his power and love not through perfect carriers, but through us. He's chosen to use we who are common, we who are fragile and easily broken, that others might see his overwhelming grace and unconditional love.

God knows the believers around you are imperfect. He knows they are weak and broken. He knows they have wounded you and oftentimes discouraged, rather than encouraged, you. But what encouragement can we find in God meeting those who are perfect? How could we possibly find hope if God only revealed himself through those without weakness? The greatest source of hope we have is that God would continuously offer grace to those who are undeserving. The greatest revelation of God's heart we have in others is that our Father never gives up on us but loves us unconditionally.

Look to others for encouragement today. Look for the kindness of God revealed through the weakness and brokenness of fellow believers. And declare the grace of God to others today, not by seeking to appear perfect, but by proclaiming the goodness of a God who would fully love someone in their imperfection. May your heart be stirred today as God's heart is revealed through the earthen vessels he's filled with his glory.

GUIDED PRAYER

1. Reflect on God's desire to reveal his heart through others.

"For what we proclaim is not ourselves, but Jesus Christ as Lord, with ourselves as your servants for Jesus' sake. For God, who said, 'Let light shine out of darkness,' has shone in our hearts to give the light of the knowledge of the glory of God in the face of Jesus Christ. But we have this treasure in jars of clay, to show that the surpassing power belongs to God and not to us." 2 Corinthians 4:5-7

2. Ask the Holy Spirit to help you see God's heart in fellow believers. Ask him to teach you to see God's grace in the imperfections and brokenness of others.

3. Choose to reveal God's heart in your life today. Choose to encourage and stir up the hearts of others by declaring God's goodness even in your brokenness.

"And let us consider how to stir up one another to love and good works, not neglecting to meet together, as is the habit of some, but encouraging one another, and all the more as you see the Day drawing near." Hebrews 10:24-25

"Each of you should use whatever gift you have received to serve others, as faithful stewards of God's grace in its various forms." 1 Peter 4:10 (NIV)

2 Corinthians 13:11 says, *"Finally, brothers, rejoice. Aim for restoration, comfort one another, agree with one another, live in peace; and the God of love and peace will be with you."* God's heart is for unity. His heart is that we would embrace one another, seek to comfort and restore one another, and thereby encounter his love and peace. Unity isn't an option in Scripture; it's a command. It's not an option to allow strife and slander. It's not an option to leave broken relationships unmended. Seek restoration today. Allow God to fill you with the courage to show love and unmerited grace to fellow believers. And as you grow in unity with others you will experience a deeper understanding of God's unconditional love and affection for you. May today be marked by a powerful revelation of God's heart through others.

Extended Reading: 2 Corinthians 4

135

A Foundation
of Affection

DEVOTIONAL

One of the most wonderful results of knowing the heart of God is living with a foundation of affection. Often we spend too much of our daily time and energy working for the affections of others. From trying to earn the respect and admiration of friends and family to vying for approval from a complete stranger, we are in constant need of affection.

But as believers we've been given a wellspring of love and affection in communion with our heavenly Father. There's nothing we have to do or could ever do to earn the love of God. His love is the beginning. His affection is meant to be the catalyst for our emotions, thoughts, and actions rather than the result. It's for this reason God calls us to be rooted and grounded in his love in Ephesians 3:17-19. Scripture says:

So that Christ may dwell in your hearts through faith— that you, being rooted and grounded in love, may have strength to comprehend with all the saints what is the breadth and length and height and depth, and to know the love of Christ that surpasses knowledge, that you may be filled with all the fullness of God.

When we seek a fresh revelation of God's unconditional love we naturally become secure and unshakable. When we discover the unfathomable depths of God's affection for us we naturally stop vying for love from others. And as we daily access the heart of God we become filled with all his fullness, richly satisfied with a love far greater than we could ever earn.

1 John 4:16 says, *"Whoever abides in love abides in God."* Take time in guided prayer to abide in the love of your heavenly Father. Let him surround you with his transcendent peace. Let him reveal his vast and overwhelming affection for you. And live today in light of God's glorious grace that you might devote your time and energy to responding to love rather than earning it. May God's affection be your foundation today.

GUIDED PRAYER

1. Meditate on the unconditional love of God available to you. Allow Scripture to fill you with a longing to be rooted in God's love.

"In this the love of God was made manifest among us, that God sent his only Son into the world, so that we might live through him. In this is love, not that we have loved God but that he loved us and sent his Son to be the propitiation for our sins." 1 John 4:9-10

2. Are you devoting time and energy to earning affection in any way? Are you seeking to earn love rather than living in response to the love you've already been given?

3. Ask the Holy Spirit to help you comprehend the breadth and length and height and depth of God's love. Open your heart to encounter and receive the unconditional love of your heavenly Father.

"So that Christ may dwell in your hearts through faith— that you, being rooted and grounded in love, may have strength to comprehend with all the saints what is the breadth and length and height and depth, and to know the love of Christ that surpasses knowledge, that you may be filled with all the fullness of God." Ephesians 3:17-19

Ephesians 5:2 says, *"And walk in love, as Christ loved us and gave himself up for us, a fragrant offering and sacrifice to God."* Live today as an act of worship to a God who's loved you to greater depths than you could ever repay. Seek to love God in all you do, think, feel, and say. Whether interacting with a stranger, eating a meal with a friend, working, walking, or breathing, do it all for the glory of your loving Father. Allow God's affection to be the foundation for your own. May your life satisfy the heart of God and stir up others around you to greater levels of devotion to our worthy King.

Extended Reading: Ephesians 3

God's Heart
Doesn't Stop with Us

DEVOTIONAL

As wonderful and life-giving as it is to access the heart of God for ourselves, having God's heart isn't meant to stop with us. His heart is meant to fill us, empower us, and transform us to live in such a way that we are light in the darkness. In Matthew 5:14-16 Jesus said:

You are the light of the world. A city set on a hill cannot be hidden. Nor do people light a lamp and put it under a basket, but on a stand, and it gives light to all in the

"Beloved, let us love one another, for love is from God, and whoever loves has been born of God and knows God."

house. In the same way, let your light shine before others, so that they may see your good works and give glory to your Father who is in heaven.

As a believer you can reveal the heart of God to others. You've been given access to a deep, revelatory knowledge of God's love that you might shine the light of God's goodness to a world that only knows darkness. You can reveal the heart of God through the way you honor rather than speaking ill. You can represent the humility of Jesus by serving rather than being self-seeking. You can reveal God's grace by offering compassion when others treat you poorly. And you can display the courage that comes from a true understanding of God's unconditional love by living authentically rather than building up a false image.

You were made to share God's heart. You were made to co-labor with him in seeing the gospel be proclaimed and bear fruit in the lives of others. Ephesians 2:10 says, *"For we are his workmanship, created in Christ Jesus for good works, which God prepared beforehand, that we should walk in them."* God has work prepared for you today. Look for opportunities to share what God is doing in your life. Look for ways you can be a reflection of the aspects of God's heart he's revealing to you. Don't let the love of God be contained to you like a secret, but share it freely, knowing that his love never runs out and is what every human heart is searching for.

Take time in guided prayer to allow God to fill you with passion to reveal his heart to a world in desperate need of restored relationship with him.

GUIDED PRAYER

1. Meditate on the importance of sharing God's heart with the world. Allow Scripture to fill you with a desire to be a reflection of God's heart.

"For we are his workmanship, created in Christ Jesus for good works, which God prepared beforehand, that we should walk in them." Ephesians 2:10

"Beloved, let us love one another, for love is from God, and whoever loves has been born of God and knows God." 1 John 4:7

"In the same way, let your light shine before others, so that they may see your good works and give glory to your Father who is in heaven." Matthew 5:16

2. What aspect of God's heart can you share with someone today? What part of God's character can you reflect to the world around you?

3. Ask the Holy Spirit to put a person or group of people on your heart that he wants you to love well today. Ask him how he wants to use you to reveal the heart of God. Journal his response.

An important aspect of sharing God's heart is trusting in faith that he will use you. When you choose to live a life co-laboring with your heavenly Father you get to experience the supernatural. It's miraculous when people choose to accept Jesus. It's astounding when our service, compassion, and love tears down walls around people's hearts that they might be more open to God. Don't just live a normal life today. Allow God to use you by sharing his heart. May your day be filled with wonder and awe at your heavenly Father who uses you in mighty and powerful ways.

Extended Reading: Matthew 5

Being a child of God

WEEK

"See what kind of love the Father has given to us, that we should be called children of God; and so we are." 1 John 3:1

WEEKLY OVERVIEW

As children of the Most High God, we have been granted access to unconditional, tangible, and perfect love. All we need we have in relationship with our Father in heaven. He longs to reveal himself to us as a loving, real Father. He longs for us to live in the fullness of restored relationship with him. He longs for us to experience his vast and limitless affections. May we grow in our understanding and experience of God as our good and loving Father this week as we look at what it is to be his child.

Fully Loved

DAY 29

DEVOTIONAL

What could true love possibly look like if not
the willing sacrifice of King Jesus for us, his
unworthy and helpless disciples? What
greater love could we possibly know than

"In this the love of God was made manifest among us, that God sent his only Son into the world, so that we might live through him. In this is love, not that we have loved God but that he loved us and sent his Son to be the propitiation for our sins."

1 JOHN 4:9-10

the love of a Father who would send his own spotless, blameless Son to die for the sins of a rebellious and prideful people? 1 John 4:9-10 says,

In this the love of God was made manifest among us, that God sent his only Son into the world, so that we might live through him. In this is love, not that we have loved God but that he loved us and sent his Son to be the propitiation for our sins.

You and I are fully, overwhelmingly, and passionately loved by our God. We have been granted access by the blood of Jesus into an eternal relationship with our Creator who considers restored relationship with us worth the death of his blameless Son. As children of God, we never again have to wonder if we are loved. God proved through the death of his Son once and for all that he will never stop pursuing us, never stop loving us, and that he will do whatever it takes to gain back what our sin took from him: a face-to-face, tangible relationship with him.

Too often we go through life wandering from person to person, possession to possession, and success to success trying to find the love we long to experience. We wake up every morning striving to

be fully loved by a world that has brokenness at the core of all it does. We search high and low for that which is already ours in Christ Jesus.

God longs to overwhelm you with his love today. He paid the highest price for you to simply experience and know the depth of his love. Isaiah 49:15-16 says, *"Can a woman forget her nursing child, that she should have no compassion on the son of her womb? Even these may forget, yet I will not forget you. Behold, I have engraved you on the palms of my hands; your walls are continually before me."* You are God's child today and forever. You are fully loved by the Creator and Lord of all. God's love is vast, limitless, and real. His affections for you know no bounds. And he is patiently waiting for you to cast aside all other pursuits of love and simply let him satisfy your need to be loved in ways far greater than you could ever imagine.

Take time in guided prayer to let God love you. Confess any ways in which you have pursued love that weren't rooted in him. Allow him to heal any wounds that have kept you from experiencing his love. And receive the incredible, vast affections your heavenly Father has for you as his beloved child.

151

GUIDED PRAYER

1. Meditate on the limitless and unconditional love your heavenly Father has for you. Allow Scripture to fill you with a desire to pursue being loved by God and to cease pursuing love from the world.

"For God so loved the world, that he gave his only Son, that whoever believes in him should not perish but have eternal life." John 3:16

"Who shall separate us from the love of Christ? Shall tribulation, or distress, or persecution, or famine, or nakedness, or danger, or sword? As it is written, 'For your sake we are being killed all the day long; we are regarded as sheep to be slaughtered.' No, in all these things we are more than conquerors through him who loved us. For I am sure that neither death nor life, nor angels nor rulers, nor things present nor things to come, nor powers, nor height nor depth, nor anything else in all creation, will be able to separate us from the love of God in Christ Jesus our Lord." Romans 8:35-39

"In this the love of God was made manifest among us, that God sent his only Son into the world, so that we might live through him. In this is love, not that we have loved God but that he loved us and sent his Son to be the propitiation for our sins." 1 John 4:9-10

2. In what ways have you pursued being loved by the world instead of God? What person have you been working to please so that they would love you? What success have you been trying to achieve to feel loved? What possession have you been trying to buy in order to feel fulfilled?

"Those who pay regard to vain idols forsake their hope of steadfast love." Jonah 2:8

3. Confess any sin of idolatry and take time to receive the conditionless affections of your Father. Ask him to show you how much he loves you. Ask him to help you receive his love in the untouched places of your heart. Rest in his presence, and allow him to lay a new foundation of grace-filled love in your life.

"So we have come to know and to believe the love that God has for us. God is love, and whoever abides in love abides in God, and God abides in him." 1 John 4:16

Often when we hear the word idolatry our minds immediately think of golden statues and other Old Testament images of false gods. The sin of idolatry is just as real and rampant today as it ever was in the days of the Old Testament. We've replaced golden statues with other possessions. We worship and place our hope in that which is fleeting and vain. Any time we value something above our God and his will we are engaging in idolatry. May we as God's children have the perspective and humility to cast down anything we've valued above him. May we repent and receive forgiveness and healing that we might serve him alone. And may we experience his love offered to us without measure and without condition.

Extended Reading: 1 John 4

New Bloodline of Freedom

DAY 30

DEVOTIONAL

To be the child of God is to be ransomed from a nature bent against God and held captive by the bonds of sin and brought into a new life freed from sin and filled with the Holy Spirit. 2 Corinthians 3:17 says, *"Now the Lord is the Spirit, and where the Spirit of the Lord is, there is freedom."* If you are a believer, you have the Holy Spirit dwelling within you. At salvation you were filled with God himself, who longs to produce the incredible fruits of righteousness and freedom instead of the sin that robs you of the abundant life afforded to you by Jesus' sacrifice.

You've been given a new bloodline of freedom. The sinful nature of Adam no longer flows through your veins. You've been made clean and given a new nature by which you can live freed from enslavement to sin. Paul writes in Romans 6:6-7, *"We know that our old self was crucified with [Jesus] in order that the body of sin might be brought to nothing, so that we would no longer be enslaved to sin. For one who has died has been set free from sin."*

In order to live each day experiencing the newfound freedom you've been given in Christ, you must spend time allowing God to give you fresh perspective. Freedom was bought for us by the blood of Jesus but is experienced through our willingness to allow God to transform and heal us. Experiencing freedom will come by allowing God to lead you away from your past mistakes and guide you into his perfect

"Beloved, we are God's children now, and what we will be has not yet appeared; but we know that when he appears we shall be like him, because we shall see him as he is. And everyone who thus hopes in him purifies himself as he is pure."

1 JOHN 3:2-3

and pleasing will. Open your heart to him and make space for him to heal the wounds that drive you to sin. Renew your mind to the new nature you've been given in Christ, and in humility depend on him for your freedom every hour of every day.

You are the child of God now. This world is no longer your home. That which you see is but a mere shadow of the incredible glory in store for you with your heavenly Father. 1 Peter 2:9 says, *"But you are a chosen race, a royal priesthood, a holy nation, a people for his own possession, that you may proclaim the excellencies of him who called you out of darkness into his marvelous light."* You belong to a new people of God who have the ability and authority to not only live free from sin but also to conquer the terrible acts of our enemy by proclaiming the powerful excellencies of our Father. You have been called out from a life of simply "getting by" into a greater pursuit of seeing God's kingdom meet the earth and transform hearts and lives for God's eternal glory.

Take time in guided prayer to allow God to give you a fresh perspective of your new bloodline of freedom. Rest in his love and lean on him for guidance and healing. May you experience a greater measure of freedom and victory today as the result of encountering the powerful love and presence of Jesus.

GUIDED PRAYER

1. Meditate on your new bloodline of freedom.
Allow Scripture to transform your perspective about who you are in Christ. Allow God's word to empower you to fight the temptations that have plagued you.

"We know that our old self was crucified with him in order that the body of sin might be brought to nothing, so that we would no longer be enslaved to sin. For one who has died has been set free from sin." Romans 6:6-7

"So you also must consider yourselves dead to sin and alive to God in Christ Jesus." Romans 6:11

"And, having been set free from sin, have become slaves of righteousness." Romans 6:18

"For freedom Christ has set us free; stand firm therefore, and do not submit again to a yoke of slavery." Galatians 5:1

2. Ask the Lord to show you a wound in your life that the enemy uses to lead you to sin. What past hurt are you trying to cover with sin? What need wasn't met? What did someone wrongly tell you?

"He heals the brokenhearted and binds up their wounds." Psalm 147:3

3. Ask the Lord to bring you freedom and healing today. Ask Jesus how he feels about whatever happened to you. Ask the Holy Spirit to guide you to the path of continual healing and freedom that you might proclaim the excellencies of your Father to a greater measure.

"For the grace of God has appeared, bringing salvation for all people, training us to renounce ungodliness and worldly passions, and to live self-controlled, upright, and godly lives in the present age, waiting for our blessed hope, the appearing of the glory of our great God and Savior Jesus Christ, who gave himself for us to redeem us from all lawlessness and to purify for himself a people for his own possession who are zealous for good works." Titus 2:11-14

Oftentimes we give into temptation because of a past experience we are trying to medicate. Those who struggle with pride are often simply trying to gain affirmation that they're good enough. Those who struggle with lust are simply trying to be loved. For every habitual sin there is a wound the Lord wants to heal. Take time to continually check your heart for wounds that are keeping you from an abundant life. Don't medicate wounds with that which will never truly heal you. Instead, allow the Spirit of God to come in and guide you to the path of healing. Your heavenly Father knows every sin you've ever dealt with and the reason that you have struggled with it. He longs to guide you into a lifestyle of freedom afforded to you by the sacrifice of Jesus. May you live out the new bloodline of freedom that is yours as the child of the Most High God.

Extended Reading: Galatians 5

Childlike Faith

DEVOTIONAL

To have faith like a child is to blindly trust the goodness, care, leadership, and provision of a father. Jesus continually called his disciples to a lifestyle of surrender and trust in him, but never so simply as in Mark 10:13-16. Scripture says,

And they were bringing children to him that he might touch them, and the disciples rebuked them. But when Jesus saw it, he was indignant and said to them, "Let the children come to me; do not hinder them, for to such belongs the kingdom of God. Truly, I say to you, whoever does not receive the kingdom of God like a child shall not enter it." And he took them in his arms and blessed them, laying his hands on them.

Mark 10 teaches that it's in having childlike faith that we will receive the kingdom of God. Childlike faith is what fills us with the unshakable hope that we will one day dwell in heaven with our Father for all of eternity. As Christians, we've placed all our hope in the truth that Jesus came, died, and rose again, and that if we place our trust in him we will have a resurrection like his. We succeed in having childlike faith when it comes to salvation, but often we fail in placing our trust in our heavenly Father on a daily basis.

Being the child of God affords us the opportunity to live under his constant provision and leadership. As our good Father, he longs to provide for us a wonderfully abundant life full of joy, peace, purpose, laughter, friends, and unconditional love. But so often we go our own way and live our lives apart from all that's available to us in God. Whether it be by a lack of revelation, impatience, fear, wrong teaching, or past experiences, we so often fail to have faith that God will shepherd us to his perfect plans.

God is calling you to a greater lifestyle of childlike faith. He is calling you to place your trust in him alone for your finances, relationships, future, past, and present. Hebrews 11:6 says, *"And without faith it is impossible to please him, for whoever would draw near to God must believe that he exists and that he rewards those who seek him."* What brings our Father pleasure is unadulterated, unveiled, and glorious relationship with his children. He longs for us to draw near to him with full assurance that he is good, real, and that he longs to bless us.

Take time in guided prayer to place your full trust in your heavenly Father. Confess to him any ways in which you have been living in your own strength. Ask him to show you the root of your lack of faith. And receive his help in pursuing a lifestyle of childlike faith. May you experience the transcendent peace and joy that only comes through living by faith.

GUIDED PRAYER

1. Meditate on the importance of having childlike faith.

"For we walk by faith, not by sight." 2 Corinthians 5:7

"And without faith it is impossible to please him, for whoever would draw near to God must believe that he exists and that he rewards those who seek him." Hebrews 11:6

"Truly, I say to you, whoever does not receive the kingdom of God like a child shall not enter it." Mark 10:15

2. Where do you struggle in trusting God? What area of your life is not producing the fruit of his goodness, reality, and love for you? Where are you under the stress of living in your own strength?

"One's pride will bring him low, but he who is lowly in spirit will obtain honor." Proverbs 29:23

3. Confess your need of God's help, and ask him to help you live with increased faith. Lay down any ways in which you've been living apart from faith, and ask the Holy Spirit to fill you with patience and trust in your heavenly Father.

"Humble yourselves, therefore, under the mighty hand of God so that at the proper time he may exalt you." 1 Peter 5:6

"The reward for humility and fear of the Lord is riches and honor and life." Proverbs 22:4

"Put on then, as God's chosen ones, holy and beloved, compassionate hearts, kindness, humility, meekness, and patience." Colossians 3:12

In speaking of Abraham, Romans 4:20-21 says, *"No unbelief made him waver concerning the promise of God, but he grew strong in his faith as he gave glory to God, fully convinced that God was able to do what he had promised."* May we be children as faithful to our good and loving heavenly Father as Abraham was. May we pursue wholeheartedly the abundant life that comes from trusting in God's reality and nearness. And may we be greater reflections of God's unconditional love and purpose for all those weary and burdened by the stress of doing life apart from the help of the Father.

Extended Reading: Romans 4

A Wealth of Fatherly Affections

DEVOTIONAL

Being the child of God gives us an open invitation into the endless affections our heavenly Father has for us. There is no end to the wealth of his love. There is no limit to how deeply and tangibly we can experience his heart. Through the sacrifice of Jesus we can live our lives totally and completely experiencing the love of the Creator and Sustainer of all.

*"Your steadfast love, O Lord, extends to the
heavens, your faithfulness to the clouds."*

PSALM 36:5

Psalm 36:5 says, *"Your steadfast love, O Lord, extends to the heavens, your faithfulness to the clouds."* When you look across the horizon as far as your eye can see, picture the arms of your heavenly Father stretching even farther than the faintest speck of blue sky. When you see the clouds in their immensity and wonder, picture the enormity of your God's faithful love toward you.

So great is the wealth of affections your heavenly Father has toward you that he would send his pure, blameless Son as payment for the sins that have kept you from experiencing his love. So great was his desire for you to know his heart that Jesus gave his life, creating a bridge across the vast chasm of sin that separated you and the Father.

1 John 4:10 says, *"In this is love, not that we have loved God but that he loved us and sent his Son to be the propitiation for our sins."* Most of us wander through life looking for any source of love we can find. We give ourselves to people, jobs, society, and wrongful expectations trying our hardest to satiate an insatiable need to be loved. Only in making time to receive God's perfect, tangible, and transformative affections will our need to be loved finally be satisfied. Only

when we look to the cross as a continual reminder that we are fully and forever loved will we stop searching for affections from a world that will only ever reject and disappoint us.

Your heavenly Father longs for you to experience the wealth of his affections today. He longs to guide you into a safe place of simply being loved by him. This broken and needy world has taught us to shield the wounded places of our hearts from any outside contact. We're taught to just get over our wounds, pick ourselves up, and let our scars be signs of our inner strength. God wants to take your wounds and heal them with his perfect love. He wants to take what the enemy meant for evil and turn it into real, eternal good. He's waiting right now to love you and make you whole. He's waiting right now to satisfy the deep longing to be loved you've carried with you all your life.

Take time in guided prayer to truly encounter the love of your heavenly Father. Wait on his presence and open your heart to him in response to his love and faithfulness. He will shepherd you to green pastures and still waters if you make time and follow his leadership. May you experience the wealth of affections your heavenly Father has for you as you pray.

GUIDED PRAYER

1. Meditate on the wealth of affections your heavenly Father has for you.

"Can a woman forget her nursing child, that she should have no compassion on the son of her womb? Even these may forget, yet I will not forget you. Behold, I have engraved you on the palms of my hands; your walls are continually before me." Isaiah 49:15-16

"In this is love, not that we have loved God but that he loved us and sent his Son to be the propitiation for our sins." 1 John 4:10

"And he arose and came to his father. But while he was still a long way off, his father saw him and felt compassion, and ran and embraced him and kissed him." Luke 15:20

2. What wound are you carrying that God longs to heal with his love? What past experience has affected you for too long? What part of your heart have you kept shielded that God longs to speak to today?

3. Ask the Lord to guide you into a transformational encounter with his love. Ask him to help you receive all the love he has to give you

today. Take time to wait on him and rest in his presence. Don't leave this place of rest until you feel satisfied and renewed.

May Ephesians 1:3-10 stir your heart to pursue the depth of affections your heavenly Father has for you throughout your day today:

Blessed be the God and Father of our Lord Jesus Christ, who has blessed us in Christ with every spiritual blessing in the heavenly places, even as he chose us in him before the foundation of the world, that we should be holy and blameless before him. In love he predestined us for adoption as sons through Jesus Christ, according to the purpose of his will, to the praise of his glorious grace, with which he has blessed us in the Beloved. In him we have redemption through his blood, the forgiveness of our trespasses, according to the riches of his grace, which he lavished upon us, in all wisdom and insight making known to us the mystery of his will, according to his purpose, which he set forth in Christ as a plan for the fullness of time, to unite all things in him, things in heaven and things on earth.

Extended Reading: Ephesians 1

God as Our Guide through Life

DAY 33

DEVOTIONAL

You were not created to carve out your path through this life alone. Your heavenly Father longs to be a guide throughout all the twists and turns of life. He longs to shepherd you to greener pastures and calmer waters. He longs to protect you and provide for you.

"I will instruct you and teach you in the way you should go; I will counsel you with my eye upon you. Be not like a horse or a mule, without understanding, which must be curbed with bit and bridle, or it will not stay near you."

PSALM 32:8-9

He longs to lead you to a life with more fullness of joy, peace, and purpose than any life you could ever discover on your own.

Proverbs 3:5-6 says, *"Trust in the Lord with all your heart, and do not lean on your own understanding. In all your ways acknowledge him, and he will make straight your paths."* Allowing the Lord to be established as your guide begins with a commitment to trust. God cannot lead where you will not follow. Unless you live life with your heart postured toward continual obedience, you will fail to follow your Father into all the wonders he has in store for you.

Psalm 32:8-9 says, *"I will instruct you and teach you in the way you should go; I will counsel you with my eye upon you. Be not like a horse or a mule, without understanding, which must be curbed with bit and bridle, or it will not stay near you."* We must cultivate a continual hunger for the Lord's instruction and counsel. God's plan is not to guide you as a horse or mule where you live your life without purpose or understanding. He longs to teach you and reveal his will that you might live under his leadership and influence.

We are created to be children of the Spirit and the word. We are made to both hear the voice of our Father and live according to the perfect direction of Scripture. John 4:24 says, *"God is spirit, and those who worship him must worship in spirit and truth."* The Holy Spirit desires to speak to you directly about your life. He longs to guide you in and out of every circumstance by tugging on your spirit and speaking to your heart. And he longs to give you revelation you need from the words of Scripture he divinely inspired. God has given you ample opportunity to be perfectly led. He's provided all you will ever need to go through life with him as your guide. All that's left is for you to trust him, keep your heart open to him, and follow him obediently in response to his faithfulness and love.

Take time in guided prayer to ask for his guidance. Ask the Holy Spirit to transform you into a child who is quick to listen and follow his leadership. Ask him to give you revelation through his word that you would be a child filled with understanding. May you encounter the desire of your Father to lead you well today.

167

GUIDED PRAYER

1. Meditate on God's desire to guide you by his Spirit and word.

"When the Spirit of truth comes, he will guide you into all the truth, for he will not speak on his own authority, but whatever he hears he will speak, and he will declare to you the things that are to come." John 16:13

"If any of you lacks wisdom, let him ask God, who gives generously to all without reproach, and it will be given him." James 1:5

"All Scripture is breathed out by God and profitable for teaching, for reproof, for correction, and for training in righteousness, that the man of God may be competent, equipped for every good work." 2 Timothy 3:16-17

2. Ask the Lord to transform you into a child quick to obey and follow his leadership. Ask him to give you great understanding of his word that you might live in accordance with Scripture.

"My sheep hear my voice, and I know them, and they follow me." John 10:27

"For a people shall dwell in Zion, in Jerusalem; you shall weep no more. He will surely be gracious to you at the sound of your cry. As soon as he hears it, he answers you. And though the Lord give you the bread of adversity and the water of affliction, yet your Teacher will not hide himself anymore, but your eyes shall see your Teacher. And your ears shall hear a word behind you, saying, 'This

168

is the way, walk in it,' when you turn to the right or when you turn to the left." Isaiah 30:19-21

"I will instruct you and teach you in the way you should go; I will counsel you with my eye upon you. Be not like a horse or a mule, without understanding, which must be curbed with bit and bridle, or it will not stay near you." Psalm 32:8-9

3. Ask the Lord about any situation in which you need guidance. Wait on him and listen intently for a response. Pay attention to what you feel peace about and what disturbs your spirit. Ask the Holy Spirit to guide you to a passage of Scripture that will give you understanding about what you should do. Pay attention to any passages or verses that come to mind.

Listening to the Lord is all about receiving in faith what God already wants to give. Our hearing is by the grace of God and not any merit of our own. God speaks to each of us perfectly. One child of God is not given more opportunity for God's guidance than another. God longs to shepherd each of us. He longs to speak to each of us. All that is required of you is to make space to listen and receive. Ask the Spirit to teach you how to listen and hold onto what he is speaking. Make space in your daily life to have dialogue with your Father. And follow his perfect leadership into the abundant life Jesus died to provide for you.

Extended Reading: Psalm 5

The Blessings of Our Father

DAY 34

DEVOTIONAL

Our Father loves to bless his children. All that we have has been given to us because our Father loves us unconditionally. In Matthew 7:7-11 Jesus says,

Ask, and it will be given to you; seek, and you will find; knock, and it will be opened to you. For everyone who asks receives, and the one who seeks finds, and to the one who knocks it will be opened. Or which one of you, if his son asks him for bread, will give him a stone? Or if he asks for a fish, will give him a serpent? If you then, who are evil, know how to give good gifts to your children, how much more will your Father who is in heaven give good things to those who ask him!

"Every good gift and every perfect gift is from above, coming down from the Father of lights with whom there is no variation or shadow due to change."

JAMES 1:17

One of the most important spiritual principles for Christians is that God is good and he gives his children good gifts. With all the depravity, pain, suffering, and wrong in the world, we must establish the unshakable goodness of our heavenly Father as our foundation. The blessings of our Father are vast and numerous. Oftentimes he blesses us in ways that go unnoticed. From a light rain or a cool breeze to an unexpected gift or miraculous healing, our God is constantly working to turn the evil in this world for our good.

James 1:17 says, *"Every good gift and every perfect gift is from above, coming down from the Father of lights with whom there is no variation or shadow due to change."* The world will try to tell you that God plays favorites. It will look at the life of one and compare it to another as if it were every person's destiny to be the wealthiest and most successful person in the world's eyes. God blesses us in far greater ways than worldly success and wealth. He is concerned with that which is eternal and will actually produce the abundant life your heart truly desires. And while provision in this world is most

definitely important and God promises to provide every thing we need physically, he has not promised to make you a success in the eyes of the world. He has only promised that if you follow him he will guide you to the best possible life filled with the fullness of relationship with him, purpose, and every spiritual blessing in the heavenly places (Ephesians 1:3).

If we truly take stock of our lives compared to what we deserve, we will begin to better see the incredible blessings given to us by our loving heavenly Father. Allow God to guide you away from the pursuit of that which is fleeting so that you might be filled with greater depths of joy at the abundance of eternal life and blessings which are yours in Christ Jesus.

Take time today to reflect on the blessings you've been given by your Father. Allow him to shift your pursuits away from earthly wealth and success toward that which will actually satisfy you for all of eternity. May you be filled with joy and thanksgiving in light of the wonderful gifts you've been given by your good and loving Father.

GUIDED PRAYER

1. Reflect on the blessings you've been given by your heavenly Father. Take time to really think about all that your God has done for you.

"Blessed be the God and Father of our Lord Jesus Christ, who has blessed us in Christ with every spiritual blessing in the heavenly places, even as he chose us in him before the foundation of the world, that we should be holy and blameless before him." Ephesians 1:3-4

"Every good gift and every perfect gift is from above, coming down from the Father of lights with whom there is no variation or shadow due to change." James 1:17

"For the Lord God is a sun and shield; the Lord bestows favor and honor. No good thing does he withhold from those who walk uprightly." Psalm 84:11

2. Ask the Lord to help you shift your pursuit away from earthly wealth and success that you might receive to greater measure the joy and blessings he longs to give you. In what ways have you been pursuing the things of the world over the things of God? What worldly pursuit has captured your attention and is guiding you away from the abundant life God longs to provide for you?

3. Take time to receive the love of your heavenly Father and rest in his presence. Often it takes spending time in God's loving presence to have our perspectives and pursuits shift. Communion with our Father changes everything.

"You make known to me the path of life; in your presence there is fullness of joy; at your right hand are pleasures forevermore." Psalm 16:11

"You will seek me and find me, when you seek me with all your heart." Jeremiah 29:13

"And he said, 'My presence will go with you, and I will give you rest.'" Exodus 33:14

When we allow God to free us from pursuing worldly success and pleasing others, we experience to greater depths the joy of relational living. When relationship with our Father is our chief goal and sole desire, we position ourselves to live joyfully and satisfied in every season and circumstance. May you follow the Lord's leadership into a life of greater joy and peace. And may your eyes be opened to the wealth of blessings given you by your loving, near, and good Father.

Extended Reading: Matthew 6

Once a Child Always a Child

DAY 35

DEVOTIONAL

As a disciple of Jesus we have full assurance of eternal, face-to-face relationship with our heavenly Father. John 10:27-30 says,

My sheep hear my voice, and I know them, and they follow me. I give them eternal life, and they will never perish, and no one will snatch them out of my hand. My Father, who has given them to me, is greater than all, and no one is able to snatch them out of the Father's hand. I and the Father are one.

"I give them eternal life, and they will never perish, and no one will snatch them out of my hand."

JOHN 10:28

Once we have become a child of God by confessing with our mouth and believing in our heart that Jesus Christ truly is Lord of all, we are the child of God forever (Romans 10:9). No sin, struggle, trial, or rebellion can pluck us from the Father's hand. And as children of God, we no longer look to this world but to our total restoration, redemption, and glorification as our source of hope.

There is peace and transcendent joy in the truth that this world is not our final resting place. Your pains and trials are temporary and pale in comparison to the incredible life that awaits you in heaven with your Father. Romans 8:38-39 says, *"For I am sure that neither death nor life, nor angels nor rulers, nor things present nor things to come, nor powers, nor height nor depth, nor anything else in all creation, will be able to separate us from the love of God in Christ Jesus our Lord."* Rest in the fact that you are fully and constantly loved by your Creator. Nothing you or anyone else could ever do has the power to pluck you from his hand. God made salvation as simple and complete as possible. Once you have been saved and brought into the kingdom of God, you are forever saved.

Titus 3:4-7 says, *"But when the goodness and loving kindness of God our Savior appeared, he saved us, not because of works done by us in righteousness, but according to his own mercy, by the washing of regeneration and renewal of the Holy Spirit, whom he poured out on us richly through Jesus Christ our Savior, so that being justified by his grace we might become heirs according to the hope of eternal life."* Your salvation is about the grace of your Father, not your own works. If salvation ever became about our own strength, it would cease to be rooted in God's loving grace and rest on our shoulders instead of the death of Jesus.

Placing our hope in eternal relationship with our Father is the path to freedom from the cares and burdens of this world. We will never truly know abundant life until we live surrendered to our King and Savior and lay the crowns and cares of this life at his feet. This world is not your home. This world is not meant to be your highest satisfaction. Pursue greater depths of relationship with your Father and watch as the stress and cares of the world fall off in light of his glorious grace. Place your hope in him alone, and follow his leading to an abundant life free from the worries, doubts, and fears that come from living for the world instead of Jesus.

175

GUIDED PRAYER

1. Meditate on God's promise of your eternal salvation as a believer. Allow Scripture to guide you to place your hope in the Father alone.

"My sheep hear my voice, and I know them, and they follow me. I give them eternal life, and they will never perish, and no one will snatch them out of my hand. My Father, who has given them to me, is greater than all, and no one is able to snatch them out of the Father's hand. I and the Father are one." John 10:27-30

"But what does it say? 'The word is near you, in your mouth and in your heart' (that is, the word of faith that we proclaim); because, if you confess with your mouth that Jesus is Lord and believe in your heart that God raised him from the dead, you will be saved. For with the heart one believes and is justified, and with the mouth one confesses and is saved." Romans 10:8-10

"For by grace you have been saved through faith. And this is not your own doing; it is the gift of God, not a result of works, so that no one may boast." Ephesians 2:8-9

2. Where have you been placing your hope? What have you been pursuing as your source of satisfaction apart from Jesus?

"Blessed is the man who trusts in the Lord, whose trust is the Lord." Jeremiah 17:7

3. Take time to confess and surrender any ways in which you have been seeking satisfaction over Jesus. Ask the Holy Spirit to help you place your hope and trust in God alone.

"'The Lord is my portion,' says my soul, 'therefore I will hope in him.'" Lamentations 3:24

"May the God of hope fill you with all joy and peace in believing, so that by the power of the Holy Spirit you may abound in hope." Romans 15:13

May Romans 5:2-5 ignite a lifestyle of continual surrender and pursuit of restored relationship with your Father:

Through him we have also obtained access by faith into this grace in which we stand, and we rejoice in hope of the glory of God. More than that, we rejoice in our sufferings, knowing that suffering produces endurance, and endurance produces character, and character produces hope, and hope does not put us to shame, because God's love has been poured into our hearts through the Holy Spirit who has been given to us.

Extended Reading: John 10